BERLITZ®

KU-770-597

ITALIAN ADRIATIC

1988/1989 Edition

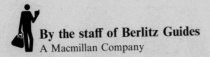

By the staff of Berlitz Guides
A Macmillan Company

6th Printing
1988/1989 Edition

PAVLO V BVRCHESIO
PONTIFICI MAXIMO
S.P.Q. ARIMINI
BENEFACTORI P
MDC.XIV

How to use our guide

- All the practical information, hints and tips that you will need before and during the trip start on page 100.
- For general background, see the sections The Region and the People, p. 6, and A Brief History, p. 12.
- All the sights to see are listed between pages 21 and 85. Our own choice of sights most highly recommended is pinpointed by the Berlitz traveller symbol.
- Entertainment, nightlife and all other leisure activities are described between pages 85 and 92, while information on restaurants and cuisine is to be found on pages 93 to 99.
- Finally, there is an index at the back of the book, pp. 126–128.

Although we make every effort to ensure the accuracy of all the information in this book, changes occur incessantly. We cannot therefore take responsibility for facts, prices, addresses and circumstances in general that are constantly subject to alteration. Our guides are updated on a regular basis as we reprint, and we are always grateful to readers who let us know of any errors, changes or serious omissions they come across.

Text: William Tuohy and Darryl Kestler
Photographer: Claude Huber
Layout: Doris Haldemann
Special thanks to Francesca Rahimi for her help on this guide.
Cartography: Falk-Verlag, Hamburg.

Maps

Italian Adriatic 21; Rimini 23; Adriatic Riviera 28; The Marches 33; Ravenna 45; Bologna 56; Veneto-Friuli 63; Venice 72

Contents

The Region and the People

If it's popular, there's a good reason why: few are the coastlines that can claim such panache, such animation, such variety as Italy's famed northern Adriatic shores.

Just what actually makes up *the* Italian Adriatic is a question of definition, for the Adriatic stretches from the top of Italy's "boot" right down to its heel. For most holiday-makers, however, it's the northern Adriatic, which starts at the Italian-Yugoslav frontier by Trieste and reaches

down to around Ancona, that holds most to offer. It encompasses four major administrative regions, that include some of Italy's most outstandingly beautiful cities—as well as some of its most attractive coastline. Friuli-Venezia Giulia in the north-east corner of Italy, long under the sway of the Austrian Empire, has its capital at Trieste. The Veneto, highlighted by the "miracle" city of Venice, runs from the Dolomites to the sea. Emilia-Romagna offers the most developed seafront, since holiday-makers have been coming to the beaches around Rimini for more than a century. And down the coast is the Marches, for many years a battleground between the Papal States and northern Italy; its capital is the thriving, broad-shouldered port of Ancona.

The whole area is influenced by the proximity of the Adriatic, a warm, soothing sea, sometimes a pale translucent blue, sometimes a rich emerald green. And the coastline is wonderfully varied: wide strands of white and beige sand alternate with coves, inlets and promontories; long sandbars, *lidi* (singular: *lido*) enclose salt-water lagoons; offshore reefs make for fascinating underwater exploration; tiny ports are crowded with brightly painted boats, serious harbours with barges and liners.

Sculptured in stone, she dreams beside the placid Brenta Canal. **7**

The mountains seem to provide a backdrop for the dramatic events that have unfolded along the coast. Many peoples have swept over it—Villanovans, Veneti, Etruscans, Romans, Franks, Goths, Huns Lombards and Byzantines and, much later, the French and Austrians—all leaving their imprint. In the early years, the tough, resourceful inhabitants vied with each other in a never-ending succession of shifting alliances and wars, building fortresses, castles and cathedrals and some of Europe's finest cities. Rich trade with the Orient brought splendour and sophistication to these cities, which shared fully in that great sunburst of artistic achievement, the Renaissance.

Great names in Italian history are connected with the Adriatic littoral: emperors Augustus and Trajan, Theodoric and Frederick Barbarossa; the powerful dukes of Sforza, Visconti, Este, Malatesta and Montefeltro; a score of popes; artists like Titian and Raphael and writers like Petrarch and Ariosto; political figures such as Garibaldi and Mussolini. Recollections of their passage here and the signs of their struggles and accomplishments can be found all over the region.

And it is this that gives the whole Italian Adriatic area its added dimension—the impressive array of cultural and historic attractions, picturesque hill-towns and splendid cities, often a mere half-hour's drive away from magnificent beaches.

Take Ravenna, for instance. For 300 years, the city was the capital of the Western Roman Empire, and the emperors commissioned the most exquisite mosaics on earth for the city's red-brick basilicas—the supreme example of Byzantine religious art that continues to dazzle today. Or, from a later period, there's Gradara, the medieval fortress setting for the tragic love story of Paolo Malatesta and Francesca da Rimini, immortalized by Dante in the *Divine Comedy*. Also high up on the list is Urbino, birthplace of the immortal Raphael, a marvellous hill-town crowned by a Renaissance masterpiece, the Ducal Palace.

Or you can drive up to San Marino, one of the smallest —and oldest—states in the

8

Ravenna's past lives on in the jewelled beauty of San Vitale.

world, to see for yourself how a toy-like nation functions, and get a superb view of the Adriatic to boot.

Behind the beaches lie stretches of cool pine woods or stands of cypress trees and, further inland, olive groves and vineyards. The gentle plains run into a rib of mountains—the Dolomites in the north, the Apennines in the south. And somewhere between the coast and the hills, you'll discover the enchanting countryside villas—like those built by master-architect Andrea Palladio. Although some of the region has been intensely developed for tourism, you can still find some patches of totally wild and unspoiled coastline. One such area is the great fan of the Po River Delta, whose misty, marshy

A crowded beach, a soothing sea but life has a serious side, too.

reaches have been turned into a national park, a refuge for birds and wildlife.

The Italians of the Adriatic are hardworking, straightforward and outgoing. They pride themselves on their independence and their natural skills. These people are old hands at tourism, and they're used to coping with the strange customs and different languages of foreigners. Their natural hospitality certainly helps make a holiday more comfortable.

The northern Adriatic coast is one of the country's finest culinary regions. Local specialities include *mortadella* sausage, *prosciutto* (ham) from San Daniele, a rich assortment of pasta and risotto, boiled meat, roast suckling pig on a spit, game birds from the marshlands. Fresh fish and shellfish, of course, are musts —broiled, fried, baked, in salad, and sometimes thrown into the pot to make *brodetto*, a delicious fish soup.

The resorts are easy to reach by car, bus, rail or air. The tourist facilities are first-class, ranging from de luxe hotels to campsites, with a large selection of comfortable accommodation in between. The weather is reliable, the sand velvety and the beach slopes gentle and safe for children. What's

more, the local communities have invested millions in purification systems to keep the water as clean as possible. Sports enthusiasts will find the necessary facilities, individualists can discover uncrowded beaches, and night people have a selection of lively after-dark spots.

11

A Brief History

From the start, Italy's Adriatic coast has been considered a plum, much sought after and fought over. Strategically located between the Alps and the Apennine mountains and the sea, it was a vital link between northern Europe, the Mediterranean world and the Orient.

The first inhabitants were probably the Villanovans, who appeared near Bologna and Ravenna about the 10th century B.C. The Veneti arrived on the coast soon afterwards. The Etruscans established several outposts in the Po Valley in the 6th century, and the Greeks founded the port of Ancona about the 4th century. It was, of course, the Romans who unified the area, setting up their regional capital at Aquileia in 181 B.C. They called the province Gallia Cisalpina and brought it into the empire in 89 B.C. Under the Pax Romana, the fertile land prospered.

Disintegration

But it was not to last. The Roman Empire began to fall apart, and the northern Adriatic coast was devastated by successive waves of invaders from across the Alps. Even in this time of turbulence, though, there were bright spots. Honorius, Emperor of the West, looking for a more secure site, moved his court to Ravenna in A.D. 402. For the next three hundred years the city shone as a brilliant centre of Byzantine art, a place where Roman and Oriental traditions came together to produce a flowering of artistic creation. Today you can still admire the basilicas and the exquisite mosaics that remain from that time.

Next it was the turn of the Lombards, a Germanic people from the Danubian provinces, to sweep southwards. By the end of the 6th century, they controlled all of northern Italy except Ravenna and its territories. In 765, they captured Ravenna, bringing to a close the Byzantine realm in Italy. In time, the Lombards converted to Catholicism and allied themselves with the pope; their ambitions in the long run, however, began to worry the latter, and he appealed for help to the Frankish king, Pepin the Short. In two campaigns, the Franks took Ravenna, Bologna, Rimini and Ancona and turned them over to Rome in the "Donation of Pepin". Pepin's son,

Charlemagne, finally beat the Lombards, and in 800 he was crowned Holy Roman Emperor by Pope Leo III.

A dark period followed for Italy, marked by constant clashes between Rome and the Germanic emperors. This enduring conflict, in the course of which neither side was able to get the upper hand and to dominate the country, left the field open to the cities, that grew rapidly, developing into important centres of economic power.

Eternally glowing mosaics were a storybook for the unlettered.

The Rise of the Cities

Foremost among the new cities was Venice, La Serenissima. From its protected position on the islands of its lagoon, Venice reaped bountiful harvests from the sea, while its ships plied the lucrative trade routes of the eastern Mediterranean. By the year 1000, Venice had established its dominion over the Adriatic after defeating the pirates of the Dalmatian coast. And with the crusades, the Venetians really struck gold, building and equipping the ships that took the knights to the Holy Land and using the knights for their own political ends. The Fourth Cru-

sade culminated in the capture and sacking of Constantinople in 1204—not one of Venice's proudest moments—after which, effectively, La Serenissima reigned supreme. The Latin Eastern Empire came thus into being and controlled all important points along the routes to Greece, Egypt and Asia Minor.

With the revival of international trade, other towns in the Adriatic region prospered and rose to prominence. Many were run by families who gave their own character to their domains. In Ferrara, it was the House of Este, in Faenza the Manfredi, in Rimini the Malatesta, in Ravenna the Da Polenta and in Urbino the Montefeltro. These petty princes did much to foster the arts. They sought out the best artists, architects and poets for

Tiny Urbino, dwarfed by the hilltop grandeur of its famous palace.

their courts in order to promote their earthly glory, and built magnificent churches to assure a place in the hereafter. It was a time of enormous creativity. In art, the stylized forms of Byzantine and Gothic began to give way to the worldly splendour of the Renaissance.

The University of Padua had been founded in 1222 by Emperor Frederick II and, by the 15th century, it was universally regarded as a great centre of learning. Dante and Petrarch studied there, and Galileo gave lectures on physics. With his discovery of the letters of Cicero, Petrarch reintroduced Antiquity to the world.

Venice's great success abroad inevitably brought it into conflict with Genoa, the other important maritime power of the day. Throughout the 14th century, the two battled. Their long and costly rivalry only came to a close with the victo-

ry of the Venetian fleet at Chioggia in 1380. Then Venice moved to expand its territory on the homefront—in Friuli and the rich valley of the Po, an initiative that was sure to provoke the Milanese. The Lombard Wars followed, lasting from 1425 to 1454. In the ensuing treaty signed at Lodi,

Sunset gilds the salty marshes of the Po Delta, known for its fish.

Milan, Venice, Florence and the pope pledged to settle their disputes by diplomatic means. This agreement resulted in a 40-year truce, the last peaceful era Italy knew for a long time.

Hard Times

For external threats darkened the horizon. On the east there were the Turks. Venice took on the role of defending Christendom against the infidels, but Constantinople fell in 1453, and the rest of Venice's eastern empire was snatched away bit by bit over the next 250 years. Then, from the north-west, came the French. Having at long last concluded the Hundred Years War with England, France was able to pull itself together and look around for other "projects". In 1494, Charles VIII invaded Italy to "claim his Neapolitan heritage". Successive monarchs followed him into Italy. After France it was the turn of Spain, and then Austria (1713). For the next three centuries, the country was buffeted by foreign powers and hardly had a history of its own.

The French Revolution had a great impact on Italy, inspiring republican sentiments that, in turn, spawned clubs and secret societies. In 1796, Napoleon crossed the Alps at the head of the French army, defeating the Sardinians and securing Nice and Savoy. He was received enthusiastically by many Italians for whom the ideals of the French Revolution spelled hope for a real Italy. But when Napoleon ceded Venice to the Austrians the following year—ending the 1,100-year-old Venetian Republic—admiration turned to disillusionment. The Cisalpine Republic was formed under French auspices in 1797 with its capital in Milan. In 1804, this became the Kingdom of Italy, with Napoleon himself wearing the ancient Lombard crown of iron.

After Napoleon's defeat in 1815, the northern regions of Italy went to Austria, constituting the Kingdom of Lombardo-Veneto. Emilia-Romagna and the Marches remained part of the Papal States. But Napoleon's influence lasted much longer than he did, for he had planted the idea of a unified Italy.

Risorgimento

The 19th century saw the rise of nationalistic movements in the country, directed against Bourbon and Hapsburg overlords. The Adriatic was infused with the spirit of Giuseppe Mazzini and Giuseppe Garibaldi, the leaders of the Risorgimento movement for Italian independence and unity. In 1848, a revolt in Venice led by Daniele Manin briefly restored the ancient republic—but when Garibaldi's relief **17** effort failed, the cause was lost. Cholera and typhus swept the city, the Austrians dropped bombs from balloons, and the Venetian nationalists were forced to capitulate 17 months later.

In 1859, war with Austria again broke out in northern Italy, resulting in the unification of Italy under Victor Emmanuel II of Piedmont in 1860. However, the Austrians still held Venetia, and the Papal States stretched along the Adriatic Marches and Romagna.

In 1866, Prussia defeated Austria, and Venetia in a plebiscite voted to join the Kingdom of Italy. Four years later, the pope was deprived of his temporal power over the Papal States, which also joined Italy. Thus the country was at last united—except for South Tyrol and Trieste.

20th Century

In World War I, Venetia and Friuli were the scene of major battles between the Italian forces and the Austrians. In October 1917, the Austrians launched a massive offensive, defeating the Italians at Caporetto on the upper Isonzo River, and driving an army of 400,000 westwards to the Piave River. But in October and November 1918, the Italians made a dramatic advance, winning a major victory at Vittorio Veneto and retaking territory just before the armistice.

In the subsequent peace conferences, Italy received the South Tyrol, up to the Brenner Pass, and Trieste.

After the war, Benito Mussolini, son of a blacksmith in Romagna, took power with his "march" on Rome in 1922 and established a Fascist state in the country. Mussolini linked Italy with Nazi Germany during World War II with disastrous results for the people. After the Italian armistice in 1943, the Germans dug in deeply to defend northern Italy. Some Adriatic cities, like Treviso, were heavily bombed, and it was not until 1945 that the Allies succeeded in capturing Rimini, Ferrara, Venice and, finally, Trieste. Mussolini was killed by partisans in 1945.

Today, the scars of war are healed, and Italy, a member of the Common Market from its inception, has climbed into the league of advanced industrial nations. In spite of a high inflation rate, in spite of social unrest and violence, in spite of political instability, the country's standard of living has constantly risen.

Art and the Cities

An energetic interchange of artists and ideas took place in Italy from the 14th to the 15th and early 16th centuries, carrying developments in the major cultural centres of Florence, Rome and Venice to the other cities. Many great figures of Renaissance art worked in the Adriatic area.

Giotto (c. 1267–1337), a Florentine, painted a series of frescoes in Padua's Cappella degli Scrovegni that profoundly marked succeeding generations of local artists. Perhaps the earliest expression of the Renaissance spirit, Giotto's work reveals a new attitude towards man and the universe.

With his heroic style and interest in antiquity, **Donatello** (1386–1466) made a great impression on his contemporaries. His *Gattamelata* equestrian statue in Padua, based on a Roman work, served as the model for monuments all over northern Italy, including **Verrocchio's** (1435–88) *Bartolomeo Colleoni* in Venice.

Piero della Francesca (c. 1415–92) worked for many years at the court of Urbino, painting the famous portraits of Federico da Montefeltro.

Urbino later saw the birth of the great High Renaissance painter **Raphael** (1483–1520), who spent most of his artistic career in Florence and Rome.

It's no accident that the figures painted by **Andrea Mantegna** (1431–1506) seem to be made of stone or bronze: the Paduan took to heart the example of Donatello. Mantegna, in turn, strongly influenced **Cosmè Tura** (1430–95), leading artist of the Ferrara School.

The Venetian **Giovanni Bellini** (1430–1516), state painter and director of a large workshop, was a master of light and colour, highly respected by the artists of his time. His most distinguished students were **Giorgione** (1478–1510), a painter of mood, and **Titian** (1490–1576). **Lorenzo Lotto** (c. 1480–1556), another Venetian influenced by Bellini, produced the best of his individualistic works in Ancona and Treviso.

In the world of architecture, **Leon Battista Alberti** (1404–72), **Donato Bramante** (1444–1514) and **Andrea Palladio** (1509–80) are the major figures from along the Adriatic. Alberti transformed a Gothic church in Rimini into the majestic classical Tempio Malatestiano; Bramante worked for the court in his native Urbino but is best known for his design for St. Peter's in Rome; Palladio centred his activities in the Veneto, enriching the area with delightful country villas, palaces and churches based on classical prototypes.

Where to Go

A tour of the northern Adriatic coast area could start practically anywhere. But perhaps the most popular stretch of the coast belongs to the province of Emilia-Romagna, the breadbasket of Italy. Known as the Romagna coast or the Adriatic Riviera, this is the focal point of many seeking a sunny Adriatic holiday. And, at the centre of it all, lies the very popular resort of Rimini.

Using Rimini and its beach area as our point of departure, we take a look at San Marino and then head down south to Ancona, visiting everything of interest on the coast and inland. Back at Rimini again, we move north to Ravenna and its riviera. At this point two major inland excursions, to Ferrara and Bologna, should not be missed. Following the coast up north into Veneto, we veer inland to Padua and the Venetian villas before arriving at Venice. A look at Treviso, and our route takes us on to the sights and coastal pleasures of Friuli-Giulia until we reach Trieste, our arrival point. But first, Rimini…

Giotto's simple, moving frescoes inspired a whole style of art.

Rimini

The Marina di Rimini extends for miles. The wide sandy beaches—at some points it's 1,000 feet from water's edge to the dunes—can accommodate thousands of bathers in relative comfort, though sociable Italians seem to welcome the proximity of others. The clean water and gently sloped beaches make Rimini ideal for children (there's even a lost-children office).

For generations, Rimini has been the leading summer resort of the Adriatic. You'll find a lively atmosphere with plenty of modern amenities—good restaurants and swinging discotheques—and the nightly promenade. Sip your coffee or drink at an outdoor café and watch the world go by.

Rimini's old town is a pleasant place to explore on foot because many streets are off-limits to cars; just watch out for the bicycles. The city is also a working fishing port, and each day you can see brightly painted boats with high bows being unloaded.

The truth of the matter is that there are two Riminis: one, the resort complex spread along the coast, with wide avenues, a multitude of hotels and well-equipped beach clubs; the other, an interesting old city steeped in history. In Roman days, Rimini was called Ariminium. A military and political centre, it lay strategically between the Via Emilia heading off towards Lombardy and Via Flaminia to Rome. And, even today, you can see the massive **triumphal arch,** in white stone from Istria, erected to honour Augustus in 27 B.C. *(Arco d'Augusto).* Also still standing—and in use—is the **Ponte di Tiberio** over the Marecchia River, the bridge which Augustus started in the last year of his life and Emperor Tiberius finished in A.D. 21.

In the 13th century, Rimini became a free city, and the forceful Malatesta family rose to power. Among the artists that visited and worked for the Malatesta court in the 15th century were Antonio Pisanello, Leon Battista Alberti, Piero della Francesca, Giovanni Bellini and Ghirlandaio. They had studied in Venice and Florence, caught the new spirit of the times and introduced the Renaissance to Rimini. After the demise of the Malatestas, Rimini fell back to the Papal States (1509). In recent times, the city played an important role in the Risorgimento, the movement for Italian independence, and became part of Italy in 1860. It was bombed heavily in World War II before being taken by the Allies in late 1944.

The main attraction in the old city is the **Tempio Malatestiano.** Originally a Franciscan church, it was magnificently redone in the Renaissance by Sigismondo Malatesta. Its stately façade by the great Florentine architect Leon Battista Alberti was inspired by the arch of Augustus. Inside, on the right, you will find the tomb of Sigismondo, the most illustrious member of the Malatesta family. The Chapel of Relics (between the first and second chapels) contains a fine **fresco** by Piero della Francesca. The tomb of Sigismondo's beloved third wife Isotta lies in the second chapel, with a **crucifix** attributed to Giotto.

At Piazza Cavour, the historical centre of Rimini, you'll find two notable buildings: the people's council once met in the 13th-century **Palazzo dell'Arengo,** with its façade of pointed arches and crenellated, biscuit-coloured brick. The Gothic **Palazzo del Podestà** now houses the Museo delle Arti Primitive, a fine collection of ethnological art.

Nearby on Via Gambalunga stands the Biblioteca Civica with the **Pinacoteca,** which, in addition to Etruscan and Ro-

man works, boasts paintings including a Pietà by Giovanni Bellini.

Just up from the Piazza Cavour lies the huge **Castello Sigismondo** on Piazza Malatesta. The impressive 15th-century structure is another legacy of Rimini's first family, the Malatestas. These two squares together form one of the best civic ensembles in Italy.

It's worth taking a few minutes to see the main shopping street, Corso di Augusto, which connects the Arco d'Augusto with the Ponte di Tiberio. On the site of the old Roman forum, now the busy Piazza Tre Martiri, Julius Cae-

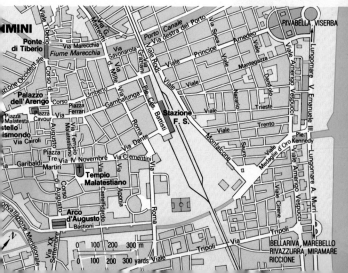

sar delivered a stirring speech after crossing the Rubicon. The 16th-century clock tower on the piazza, Torre dell'Orologio, still marks the hours. Several blocks to the east you'll find the remains of the Roman amphitheatre.

Near Rimini, there are two **adventure parks** to amuse the kids. One, at Viserba, is a miniature reconstruction of the Italian peninsula with its most famous monuments. The other, Fiabilandia at Rivazzur-ra, is a kind of Disney World with a Far West Village, a Pinocchio's World, and so on.

Moving south from the centre of Rimini, you'll come across beach areas that are part of the city—BELLARI-VA, MAREBELLO, RIVAZZURRA and MIRAMARE—with city buses running just behind the beaches.

An enigmatic, excommunicate noble created the Malatesta Temple.

San Marino to Loreto

The Republic of San Marino

High above the Adriatic coast, a half-hour's drive from Rimini, lies the smallest and oldest republic in the world—San Marino. The pocket-sized nation—a 24-square mile patch with its capital town perched on the three-peaked pinnacle of Monte Titano—was founded more than 1,500 years ago. The story goes that a Dalmatian stonecutter named Marinus fled here to escape religious persecution from the Romans. He was subsequently canonized, hence the derivation of the name.

The San Marinese fortified the three peaks of their summit and followed the Roman system of electing two consuls as heads of state. Partly because of its crow's-nest location, it stayed clear of the wars and invasions that ravaged Italy, and aside from a brief spell under Cesare Borgia, the republic succeeded in maintaining its independence. Eventually, it accepted the sovereignty of the Kingdom of Italy and then the Italian Republic. Though San Marino stayed neutral in World War II, it was bombed even so.

Today, there are close to 20,000 citizens of San Marino. The republic has its own army, a blue-and-white flag, it mints coins and prints stamps and issues its own licence plates, "RSM". Some 35 countries, including the Soviet Union and the People's Republic of China, maintain diplomatic relations with San Marino.

The government of San Marino is headed by two "regent captains", who hold office jointly for six months. Their investiture takes place each year on April 1 and October 1 in a colourful ceremony.

On the main square, Piazza della Libertà, are the Florentine-Gothic-style Palazzo Pubblico, which houses the 60-member Grand Council, and the Basilica di San Marino, a 19th-century neo-classical building where St. Marinus is buried.

Inside the palace hangs a large portrait of Antonio Onofri, a foreign secretary sometimes called the "saviour of the country". He was the one to refuse Napoleon's offer of additional territory at the expense of Italy and for this reason—and this alone—after the emperor's downfall, San Marino was allowed to retain its special status.

The 14th-century church of **25**

San Francesco contains a small art gallery, with a *St. Francis* by Guercino and a *Madonna and Child* attributed to Raphael. In the Museo e Pinacoteca Governativi, you'll see good examples of the local painters, as well as Etruscan pieces and mementoes of Garibaldi's stay here in 1849.

But by far the most impressive sight in San Marino is the superb **view** of the Adriatic, the Apennines and the Po Valley. And it's best from the three "towers"—Rocca Guaita, Cesta and Montale—that are the symbol of the republic.

South of Rimini

The first major resort south of Rimini is **Riccione**—which ranks among the most popular in Europe. Referred to by city fathers as "The Green Pearl of the Adriatic", Riccione has $3^1/_2$ miles of inviting beaches backed by verdant parks and a picturesque centre. During the summer months, they hold art, literary and stamp-collecting festivals and set off fireworks at night to spice up the seaside life.

Riccione has dozens of large and small hotels, pensions and other accommodation from the luxurious to the most simple. Mussolini used to spend his summers here, but his

family villa has been demolished and the site turned into a public garden. The resort is near Miramare Airport, serving Rimini and the Adriatic Riviera.

Further down the coast is MISANO ADRIATICO, a rapidly expanding resort on the "Riviera del Sole" (Riviera of the

Southern sun pours a warm libation on popular Cattolica beach.

Sun), with a backdrop of steep hills. Here you can choose a villa or hotel either on the sea, or up above on the hills, with a wonderful view. The hills also offer the visitor the prospect of pleasant, shaded walks—sometimes a welcome change from sand and sun.

The most southerly resort on the Adriatic Riviera is **Cattolica,** a well-established beach community 20 kilometres south of Rimini. Its name derives from the orthodox Catholic bishops who found **27**

refuge here in 359 during the Council of Rimini. Holiday-makers enjoy Cattolica's wide strand, set on an attractive bay surrounded by hills. The town is quieter than Rimini with a high proportion of families who return year after year. It claims the most equable climate along the coast, and its popularity is reflected in its constant expansion.

The Marches

The region of the Marches begins just south of San Marino and stretches down, between the Apennines and the Adriatic coast, to the River Tronto.

Close to the coast, you'll find the fairy-tale castle of **Gradara,** a 14th-century fortress built by the Grifi and inhabited in turn by the Malatesta and the Sforza. This was the site of the tragic romance between Francesca da Rimini and her brother-in-law, Paolo Malatesta. The lovers were discovered one evening by Francesca's husband, Gianni, who returned unexpectedly. He murdered the adulterous couple, but Dante immortalized them in the *Inferno.* A popular legend asserts that if you see Francesca's shadow wandering over the wall of the castle on the night of the full moon, you will have good luck in love. Because of its altitude and cool climate, Gradara is a popular spot on hot summer nights.

Down below is the seaside resort of GABICCE MARE, where holiday-makers relax under gaily coloured parasols by day and enjoy the lively music by night. If you're heading south to Pesaro, follow the **panoramic route** along the coast. It winds around through maritime pines and cypress trees, passing isolated hill-towns, fine villas and offering superb glimpses of the sea.

Pesaro, site of the old Roman port of Pisaurum, was the birthplace of opera composer Gioacchino Rossini (1792–1868). At various times during the Renaissance, the town was ruled by the prominent Malatesta, Sforza and Della Rovere families. In 1631, it became part of the Papal States.

Pesaro combines pleasant wide beaches and esplanades with an active port and some fine medieval monuments. Overlooking the Piazza del Popolo is the arcaded **Palazzo Ducale,** started by Alessandro Sforza around 1450. Near the sea you'll find the Rocca Costanza, an imposing fortress built by the Dalmatian Laurana for Costanzo Sforza in the 15th century.

The Via Rossini goes by the composer's unassuming house, now a museum, to the cathedral with its Romanesque-Gothic portal. Don't miss the **Musei Civici,** which has some marvellous primitive paintings. Highlights include the *Pala di Pesaro* and *Crucifixion* of Giovanni Bellini. The museum's ceramics collection is outstanding, especially the Umbrian pottery. And in the nearby Museo Archeologico Oliveriano, on Via Mazza, you'll see an interesting array of Etruscan artefacts.

At the north-east end of the Via Flaminia (about 10 kilometres south of Pesaro) lies the old fishing port of **Fano,** now a flourishing resort with long beaches. The town was the site of the Roman colony of Fanum Fortunae, which took its name from a temple of fortune erected by the Romans after they defeated Hannibal's brother in 207 B.C.

Fano is a pleasant place to stroll about, with pedestrian malls, Roman walls, a picturesque fishing canal-port—and beautiful women. At least that's what they say locally, claiming that the women of Fano are the prettiest in Italy.

You'll enjoy the old town with its cobblestone streets and the **Arco di Augusto** from the

1st century A.D. Note the arcaded Loggia di San Michele nearby, built in part with stones from the arch. The former church of San Michele has a beautiful façade with portals by Bernardino da Carona (1512).

In the centre of town, on Piazza XX Settembre, you'll see the symbol of Fano, the 16th-century Fountain of Fortune. Also on the square: the Romanesque-Gothic Palazzo della Ragione and the Palazzo Malatesta, which houses the municipal museum and an art gallery.

At the northern corner of the old walled city, you'll find the Rocca Malatestiana, an imposing fortress built according to a design by Sigismondo Malatesta in the 15th century.

The Fano Riviera begins with the resort of TORRETTE, a small but growing beach community preferred by families. Not so long ago, it had only one hotel with two small towers, hence the name "Torrette". To the south, MAROTTA is a lively town with a commercial fishing port. In April, the fishermen here celebrate the festival of the *garagoi*, or molluscs, which are cooked in aromatic sauces made with olive oil, tomatoes and herbs—a fine civic treat.

The major resort on this stretch is SENIGALLIA, known for its "velvet beach"—almost 4 miles of it—backed by a promenade lined with hotels and residences. Senigallia was fought over many times, to such an extent that Dante called it the quintessential "ruined city". The dominant structure today is the fortress that Baccio Pontelli built in the late 15th century for Giovanni Della Rovere.

Three kilometres west of Senigallia you'll find the Renaissance church of Santa Maria delle Grazie, probably also the work of Pontelli, with a *Madonna and Saints* by Perugino.

If you don't leave the beach for a few hours to venture into the hills behind the Marches coast, you'll miss something very special. Inland, there are picturesque hill-towns, fortified castles, monasteries, rolling countryside and a completely different atmosphere. From the Camaldolese abbey of EREMO DI MONTE GIOVE (5 kilometres south-west of Fano), you can enjoy a fine view of the Metauro Valley. SANT'ANGELO IN LIZZOLA has **31**

Inland from Rimini, golden hillsides look over peaceful valleys.

old walls and towers and a charming baroque church; EREMO DEL BEATO SANTO, founded by the Order of St. Francis in the 13th century, is a site of pilgrimage. In SAN

All the fearsome fun of the fair when it's Carnival time in Fano.

COSTANZO, there's a medieval castle, as well as a polenta festival on the first Sunday of Lent. MONDAVIO, further inland, also has a fortified castle, but of Renaissance vintage. In FOSSOMBRONE, you'll find the remnants of an ancient Roman forum, a number of palaces, and the sumptuous residence of the dukes of Urbino, now the Museo Civico.

Urbino

Urbino (37 kilometres from Pesaro), queen of the hill-towns, is a must on the list of any visitor interested in Italian art and history. It was the home of the Montefeltro family, which ruled the city from the 12th until the early 16th century.

During the reign of Federico da Montefeltro (1442–82), a militaristic but enlightened prince, the court was one of the great humanist centres of Europe. Urbino's artists—Giovanni Santi, his son Raphael, Federico Barocci and architect Bramante—gained fame far beyond the city. Federico also attracted great talent from outside to his court. He commissioned Piero della Francesca to paint the remarkable portraits of himself and his wife, and brought in Dalmatian architect Luciano Laurana to complete the palace. In addition, Federico assembled the most magnificent library of his time.

During World War II, the town served as a repository of art from all over Italy, and the old fortifications held firm throughout the German occupation.

Dominating Urbino and the surrounding hills, the **Palazzo Ducale** has become the symbol of the city. This masterpiece of Renaissance architecture was built around two old Gothic palaces. The façade is a mixture of cream-coloured Dalmatian limestone and russet brick. On the western side two turreted round towers enclose superimposed loggias. Taken all together, many seemingly disparate elements blend into a graceful entity. Inside, the elegantly proportioned rooms surround an arcaded courtyard, a superb example of the harmonious, balanced Renaissance style.

Today, the Ducal Palace has been turned into a museum, the **Galleria Nazionale delle Marche** (National Gallery of the Marches) with its works beautifully displayed. Among the outstanding paintings you'll see are a *Madonna* by Andrea Verrocchio, the *Profanation of the Host* by Paolo Uccello, the *Flagellation* and *Madonna of Senigallia* by

THE MARCHES

Piero della Francesca, a portrait of a woman, known as *The Mute*, by Raphael. The most amazing room in the palace, however, is the dukes' study or **Studiolo**, which is completely covered with pictures in inlaid wood, some from designs by Botticelli.

In 1975, Italians were horrified to hear that thieves had stolen the Raphael portrait and della Francesca's *Flagellation* and *Madonna*. When the works were recovered the following year, the church bells rang out from every campanile in Urbino.

On the piazza in front of the palace, you'll find the church of San Domenico, with a fine Renaissance portal, and the Duomo, which contains several paintings by Barocci. It's worth seeking out the **Oratorio di San Giovanni Battisti** on Via Barocci for the intriguing frescoes of the life of St. John the Baptist by Lorenzo and Iacopo Salimbeni (1416).

Urbino's steep, narrow streets are delightful. At any turn you may come upon a graceful courtyard, a fine loggia, an unexpected perspective or the landscape suddenly opening up in the distance. On Via Raffaello you'll find the small **house** where Raphael lived for the first 14 years of his life. It contains the great painter's memorabilia and one of his first paintings, a *Madonna*. After exploring the town, climb up to the ramparts. From almost any point, the **views** are superb—of the Ducal Palace and surrounding buildings, and of the mountains and lovely countryside around Urbino.

Ancona and the Riviera del Conero

After passing a string of beaches marred by an oil refinery, you come to **Ancona**, capital of the Marches. Beautifully set on a promontory above the sea, it's an important seaport, bustling with ferry traffic to Greece and Yugoslavia; and indeed, it's the only port on the Adriatic of international significance between Venice and Bari.

The whole history of Ancona has been tied to the sea. Founded by Greek colonists from Syracuse in the 4th century B.C., it was called Ankon (an elbow) because of its position jutting out from the Adriatic coast. Ancona prospered as a Roman port and later

34

Urbino's Ducal Palace: restraint without, a feast of art within.

belonged to the Ravenna Exarchate (the exarch was the viceroy of the Byzantine emperors). It eventually became a free city under papal protection.

In recent times, Ancona was bombarded by the Austrian fleet in World War I, occupied by the Germans in World War II and bombed by the Allies before being taken by the Poles in 1944. Since then, the town, which lies on a fault line, has suffered much damage from earthquakes, and public buildings are often temporarily closed to the public; check at the tourist office before visiting.

In spite of its battered history, the city has a certain elegance. Start off your visit with the powerful-looking **Duomo** dedicated to St. Cyriacus, one of the early Christian bishops of Ancona. Built on the site of a temple of Venus, the church incorporates Byzantine and Romanesque styles and has a 12-sided cupola, one of the oldest in Italy. The interior is quite simple and dignified.

From the terrace outside, you overlook the port and the **Arco di Traiano** (Trajan's Arch), erected in A.D. 115 in honour of the Roman emperor who "modernized" the harbour.

Also worth seeing in Ancona is the elaborate early 13th-century façade of Santa Maria della Piazza with intriguing carvings of animals and people. Some beautiful examples of Venetian Gothic, to which the Dalmatian sculptor Giorgio Orsini (Jurag Dalmatinac) contributed, are the church of San Francesco, the Portale di Sant'Agostino and the Loggia dei Mercanti with its statues of the Virtues. In the Palazzo Ferretti there's the National

Museum of the Marches and in the Palazzo Comunale, an art gallery with a good collection of local artists.

South of Ancona, the **Riviera del Conero** extends along the rocky coast, a series of inlets, grottoes and lovely little beaches. The sea here, one of the best places in the Adriatic for underwater fishing, ranges from dark green to violet. You'll find three villages here reminiscent of those along the Amalfi coast: PORTONOVO, with its exquisite Romanesque church, Santa Maria di Portonovo; SIROLO, surrounded by pine woods; and NUMANA, which has a sanctuary, Santuario del Crocifisso, with a valuable Byzantine crucifix. Each of the towns has small beaches hollowed out of the white limestone cliffs.

Midday brings a timeless quiet to Ancona, for 2,000 years one of the busiest ports on the Adriatic.

Beach umbrellas await the heat of the day to unfurl their colours.

In the hills behind Ancona, there's a sprinkling of villages that are worth visiting when you're in the mood for a drive. The closest is CAMERANO, a market town whose main industry is making accordions. Above, Monte Conero commands a marvellous panorama of the Apennines and the Adriatic.

Not far inland, you'll discover the walled town of OSIMO, once Auximum, the 5th-century city of the Picenes. The Duomo, which goes back to the 13th century, has a handsome façade and a splendid bronze font in its baptistry by the Iacometti (1627).

The Emperor Frederick II (1194–1250) and composer G.B. Pergolesi (1710–36) were both born in the walled town of **Iesi**. With its central piazza surrounded by a harmonious

 east of Ancona is the world-famous sanctuary in **Loreto**, dedicated to the Virgin Mary. According to tradition, the house where Mary was born and where Jesus lived was spirited away from Nazareth by angels and set down on the hill of Trsat in Dalmatia in 1291. Three years later, the Holy House was moved again, this time across the Adriatic to a deserted hill near Ancona. At first there was only a simple courtyard with arcades around the Santa Casa (Holy House), but with the advent of pilgrims an elaborate sanctuary was built. From the laurel covering the hill came the name of Loreto.

You enter the Piazza della Madonna through an archway. In the centre there's an immense 17th-century fountain; on one side the handsome unfinished Palazzo Apostolico, begun by Bramante and Andrea Sansovino. Inside, you'll find a *pinacoteca* with some works by Lorenzo Lotto and Brussels tapestries based on drawings by Raphael.

The **Santuario della Santa Casa** is a basilica of heroic proportions, and with its ramparts it looks like a fortified church. Started in Gothic style in 1468, the church was continued by Renaissance architects **39**

ensemble of churches and public buildings, Iesi resembles a Tuscan hill-town. The finest building here is the Renaissance **Palazzo della Signoria,** designed by Francesco di Giorgio Martini, a pupil of Brunelleschi. The art gallery inside the palace has some of the best paintings of Venetian artist Lorenzo Lotto. Don't leave without trying the crisp white wine of Verdicchio that is produced around Iesi.

About 30 kilometres south-

—among others, Benedetto and Giuliano da Maiano, Baccio Pontelli, Bramante and Sansovino. Bramante added the side chapels in 1511, Vanvitelli the lofty domed campanile in 1750. The simple late-Renaissance façade features magnificent bronze doors, adorned with statues of the prophets and Biblical scenes. On the steps is a statue of Pope Sixtus V, who had Loreto fortified.

You'll find the interior of the basilica somewhat gloomy —which only adds to the air of mystery. The Santa Casa itself stands under the dome. The inside is quite plain, but the exterior has been faced with elegant marble designed by Bramante, with bas-reliefs and statues by Sansovino and others. Some of the scenes relate the removal of the Holy

She has seen pilgrims in their hundreds, honouring Loreto's Holy House and Renaissance sanctuary.

House; others depict episodes in the life of Mary. They say that the stones inside—now blackened by the smoke of votive candles—are not at all like local material but bear a striking resemblance to that used in Palestine 2,000 years ago.

The four sacristies of the basilica are sumptuously decorated: St. John's has a tiled floor, a fine lavabo and frescoes by Luca Signorelli; St. Mark's boasts a cupola with frescoes by Melozzo da Forlì.

Don't leave Loreto without having seen the **view** from behind the basilica—of the Adriatic to the east and the Conero Massif to the north.

Pilgrim's Progression

Loreto has been a magnet to the faithful for five centuries. In 1493, Columbus' crew made a vow to the Madonna of Loreto during a storm on the Atlantic. Popes soon began including the shrine on their itineraries, as did scientists and philosophers like Galileo and Descartes. Mozart is supposed to have played the organ in the basilica at the age of 13, improvising preludes and fugues.

In 1920, Pope Benedict XV proclaimed the Madonna of Loreto the patroness of avia-

tion, which is why American astronaut Edward McDivitt carried the Madonna's medallion along on his flight to the moon.

Trains from all over Italy pour into Loreto bearing pilgrims. And the whole town is devoted to taking care of them. The most important pilgrimage dates are the Annunciation, March 25th; Assumption, August 15th; Nativity, September 8th; and the Journey of the Santa Casa on December 10th.

Rimini to Pomposa

North to Ravenna

The first few beaches north of Rimini, like those to the south, are extensions of the city's seafront: SAN GIULIANO A MARE, across the canal port, RIVABELLA, north of the Marecchia River, VISERBA, VISERBELLA and TORRE PEDRERA. They are practically indistinguishable from one another, offering dozens of small hotels and pensions within walking distance of the broad, flat beach, as well as bus service to the centre of Rimini.

Further on you'll find the twin resorts of IGEA MARINA, named after Hygieia, the Greek and Roman goddess of health, and BELLARIA. A long breakwater helps make the sea calm and warm in this area, stretching the season from May to October. Bellaria has ancient origins and a respectable 14th-century fortress, Castrum Lusi. There is also a Saracen tower which now houses a museum with exotic shells and a numismatic collection. The resorts have their own

Vivid sails almost outdazzle the sun in Cesenatico's fishing port.

shops, an open-air market and restaurants, independent of Rimini.

Moving north to the Rubicon, you'll come to SAN MAURO A MARE, a small community of seaside cottages with large dunes between the pine woods and the Adriatic. On the other side of the famous river—that Caesar crossed with his troops in 49 B.C., violating a prohibition and upsetting Pompey immeasurably—the wide beach resort of GATTEO A MARE enjoys a reputation for peace and quiet. Both VILLAMARINA and VALVERDE beyond are new and still growing.

The first major resort north of Rimini, **Cesenatico,** was built as a harbour for the inland town of Cesena in 1502 by Cesare Borgia, supposedly on the basis of plans drawn up by Leonardo da Vinci. Cesenatico's wide expanse of soft sand and calm sea should help you overlook the skyscrapers standing at the water's edge. The town bubbles with life and has broad streets shaded by umbrella pines. At the picturesque canal port, you'll see the local fishing boats, *bragozzi,* with their brightly coloured sails. The old town has good shopping.

Just north are the new beach resorts of ZADINA PINETA and PINARELLA. They're satellites of **Cervia,** a modern complex with bathing establishments and campsites, plenty of hotels, villas and cottages. Cervia also has major spa facilities, with mud baths and hydrotherapy —excellent for rhumatic and arthritic complaints, among others. On Ascension Day, they celebrate a "Wedding of the Sea" here in which the bishop throws his ring into the Adriatic. The name Cervia comes from the deer (*cervo* in Italian) who roam the grounds of a large local park.

Adjoining Cervia and forming virtually part of it is one of the most fashionable spas on the Adriatic Riviera—**Milano Marittima,** a favourite resort of the Milanese. Many of the villas here are secluded among the dense pine trees, giving the resort a rustic air. Riding enthusiasts are particularly well catered for.

LIDO DI SAVIO, a rapidly developing resort at the mouth of the Savio River, is connected by road to Milano Marittima. Across the river, LIDO DI CLASSE, with its recently built hotels and flats, has an unfinished look. The busy port canal serves as the outlet for the nearby salt pans.

While these new beach resorts cannot claim historic mo- **43** numents, they do offer a quiet relaxing atmosphere among the pine trees by the sand and sea, plus good facilities for such sports as riding, tennis and golf.

Ravenna

Once the capital of the Byzantine Empire of the West, Ravenna continues to live in the shadow of its past glories, and has weathered the passage of time remarkably well. Today this city of red brick and tiled roofs boasts the finest examples of Byzantine architecture in Italy—the basilicas of San Vitale and Sant'Apollinare Nuovo.

Although it now lies some 10 kilometres inland, Ravenna was a flourishing seaport under the Romans—250 ships could anchor there at a time. It rose to prominence when Honorius chose it as the capital of the Western Empire in 402. He was succeeded by his sister, Galla Placidia, who enriched the city with monuments. The Goths also established their court here, first Odoacre (in 476) and then Theodoric (493–526), a tough, enlightened ruler, who built extensively. In 540, the Byzantine general Belisarius captured Ravenna for Justinian, under whose rule the city enjoyed a brilliant period of artistic creation, strongly influenced by Eastern tradition.

Start your tour of Ravenna with the **Mausoleo di Galla Placidia.** Built in the second quarter of the 5th century in the form of a Greek Cross, the small chapel contains superb mosaics, probably the city's oldest. The colours are extraordinary, especially the deep blue. The mosaics depict the Good Shepherd, St. Laurence, the Apostles and Evangelists, while overhead the night sky of the dome is studded with golden stars that seem to sparkle with their own light.

Next to the mausoleum is the basilica of **San Vitale,** an octagonal structure founded by Bishop Ecclesius (526) and consecrated in 547–48. The plain red-brick exterior gives you little indication of the ravishing treasures inside, for the magnificent green and gold **mosaics** in the choir and apse are unrivalled. They represent scenes from the Old Testament, and there are two famous panels of the Emperor Justinian and his Empress Theodora surrounded by members of their court. The dome of the apse shows Christ between two angels with St. Vitale and Bishop Ecclesius, who holds a model of the

church. Eight marble pillars support the Byzantine dome of the basilica with its *matroneum*, or women's gallery.

The adjoining **Museo Nazionale** occupies the cloisters of the ancient San Vitale convent. In the two courtyards, you can see Roman, Early Christian and Byzantine sculptures. Also displayed are a collection of ceramics, icons, medals, arms and fabrics.

Another mosaic-filled gem is the **Battistero Neoniano** near the cathedral, formerly known as Neone degli Ortodossi. The domed octagonal building, originally a Roman bath house, is crowned by mosaics from about 450 of the Baptism of Christ surrounded by an evocative procession of the Twelve Apostles.

The basilica of **Sant'Apollinare Nuovo** dates from the time of Theodoric (early 6th century). The mosaics on the walls of the nave, executed in classical Byzantine style, depict the life and passion of Christ; on the left you'll see a procession of virgins, on the right, the martyrs, all with jewelled crowns in hand.

The **Battistero degli Ariani** on the Piazza Ariani, from the 5th–6th centuries, originally belonged to the Arian Goths (those Germanic tribes that **45**

The Glory of Ravenna

The mosaics of Ravenna have withstood the years in extraordinary condition. Composed of tiny cubes *(tesserae)* set irregularly to reflect the light, these masterworks lining the brick walls of the city's churches are so luminous they seem to transform the architecture.

The idea of decorating a surface with small, closely set pieces of stone, glass, shell or metal may have originated with Stone Age man. Mosaics have been found at Egyptian and Minoan sites. The Greeks and Romans greatly improved the technique, for the most part in floor mosaics of vari-coloured marble cubes depicting mythological or hunting scenes, but the art form reached its height during the Byzantine era in Ravenna.

Most of Ravenna's mosaics are made of coloured glass, mother-of-pearl and gold leaf placed on the underside of clear glass cubes. You can trace the progression from the early naturalism of the Mausoleum of Galla Placidia—still under the influence of the Hellenic-Roman tradition—to the formalized Byzantine style of San Vitale. Both early and late mosaics share the harmony and vivacity of colour, the rhythm of the design and an incredible luminosity.

adhered to Arianism, a religion which denied the divinity of Jesus). Its fine mosaics show the Baptism of Christ and the Twelve Apostles.

The Venetian influence will strike you in the city's principal square, **Piazza del Popolo.** The main building looks like a small version of the Doges' Palace in Venice, and two

Humble and kingly, Sant'Apollinare's Magi hasten on with gifts.

Venetian columns bear Ravenna's patron saints, Apollinare and Vitale.

In the centre of the old town, you'll find the **Tomba di Dante.** The poet, exiled from his native Florence, finished writing the *Divine Comedy* in Ravenna, where he died in 1321. The monument, erected in 1780, covers an older structure housing his sarcophagus.

The circular **Mausoleo di Teodorico** (526) on the outskirts of town is a curious edifice composed of huge blocks of limestone that were floated across the Adriatic from Istria. The dome, 37 feet in diameter, was carved from a single stone, weighing about 300 tons. Nobody has figured out how they managed such a construction feat.

Some 5 kilometres south-east of Ravenna is the best example of a Romanesque basilica in Italy, the stately **Sant'Apollinare in Classe** (549). The round campanile

with windows on each storey was added in the 11th century. The interior of the church with two arcades supported by marble columns conveys an exalted sense of space, light and grace. You'll also see lovely **mosaics,** touching in their naïvity and serenity, predominantly in green, blue and white. In the apse is the Transfiguration, with St. Apollinare, first martyr and bishop of Ravenna, surrounded by sheep (the chosen ones) on a beautiful green meadow. Above are various biblical figures with a large cross (Christ) at the summit.

Extending down towards the sea from Sant'Apollinare in Classe, you'll find the very old and very famous **Pineta di Classe.** From Dante to Byron, poets sung the praises of this majestuous wood, now alas threatened by sprawling development.

Today a school of mosaics carries on Ravenna's rich tradition. You can also visit the studios of artisans, who execute mosaic panels based on 5th- and 6th-century motifs or on sketches provided by modern artists.

Sant'Apollinare in Classe is set in a landscape of field and tree.

Faenza

Anyone interested in ceramics should definitely visit Faenza, 31 kilometres inland, the city that gave its name to the famous bright and attractive pottery known as *faïence* or majolica.

It is thought that the Italian potters learned their art from the Majorcans (who, in turn, learned it from the Arabs), but in any case their work here around Faenza reached its height in the 15th and 16th centuries. In the town's magnificent **Museo Internazionale delle Ceramiche,** you can not only see some fine examples of this special style of pottery from this era up to the present, but also pre-Columbian and contemporary pieces by such artists as Picasso, Matisse and Chagall.

Faenza, birthplace of the inventor of the barometer, Evangelista Torricelli (1608–47), has two spacious piazzas around which the city's major buildings are grouped. On Piazza della Libertà, you'll see the **Duomo,** begun in 1474 by Giuliano da Maiano; its façade was never finished. The Piazza del Popolo has the city clock tower, the town hall, once the palace of the Manfredi family, and the 12th-century Palazzo del Podestà.

Ravenna Riviera and Northwards

Returning now to the sea, a succession of beach resorts string themselves out along the Ravenna Riviera. All offer broad stretches of sandy beach, modern facilities, a holiday atmosphere; a few unfortunately face onto industrial developments—but there's always the sea nearby…

The first, LIDO ADRIANO, is due east. Heading north, PUNTA MARINA has acquired a solid reputation as a thermal spa, with a skilled staff to provide iodine hydrotherapy and mud baths.

The largest resort on this coast is MARINA DI RAVENNA, which has grown up around busy PORTO CORSINI. The area has plenty of good restaurants and well-equipped bathing establishments among the pines. On the other side of the Candiano Canal, linking Ravenna to the sea, you'll find MARINA ROMEA. Small lakes behind the beach are being developed for water-skiing and boating. Fittingly for the region, there's a mosaic school here in the summer. The last stop on the Ravenna Riviera, CASAL BORSETTI, is fairly new, but its lively canal-port adds some colour.

Across the Reno River are 12 more miles of seaside towns in the province of Ferrara. LIDO DI SPINA features an unusual chair-lift that swings bathers across the dunes from the town to the beach. LIDO DEGLI ESTENSI, the oldest of the Ferrara resorts, has well-developed facilities with a good assortment of restaurants, bars and night spots on its brightly lit avenues. You'll also find a good small-boat harbour and a water-skiing school.

Next comes PORTO GARI-BALDI, where the Italian patriot landed in his ill-fated attempt to take Venice in 1849. The town, destroyed in air raids during World War II, has been totally rebuilt. The new resort of LIDO DEGLI SCACCHI, to the north, is popular with campers as well as bathers. LIDO DI POMPOSA takes its name from the nearby abbey, and LIDO DELLE NAZIONI has developed into a rather "classy" resort, with an artificial lake behind the beach for water sports. The northernmost of this group of coastal towns is LIDO DI VOLANO. Its long beach backed by pinewoods stretches towards the Po River Delta.

Set back a few miles from the beach, the amusing village of **Comacchio** is built on 13 little islands set in a lagoon. With its network of canals and bridges and its fishermen's houses, it looks like a tiny Venice. Don't fail to cross the Trepponti, a charming bridge built in 1634 at the intersection of several canals. The inhabitants of Comacchio are mainly engaged in the catching and curing of eels.

West of Comacchio lie the ruins of SPINA, an Etruscan city that carried on a profitable trade with Greece. Founded about 530 B.C., the town's heyday was brief, and within 300 years it had faded into oblivion. Aerial surveys helped archaeologists locate the remains of the city, however, and excavations, begun in 1956, revealed Spina to be an important Etruscan necropolis. The beautiful pottery found here is now housed in the archaeological museum of Ferrara.

Beyond Comacchio, on the east side of the road to Venice, is the Benedictine abbey of **Pomposa,** a masterpiece of Romanesque art. The **church,** with its walls decorated with frescoes dating back to the 8th–9th centuries, follows the Ravenna style. Its façade is decorated with Byzantine motifs. The church, the majestic, windowed **campanile,** the cloisters and refectory form a harmonious architectural ensemble. It was at Pomposa, a great centre of culture in the Middle Ages, that the monk Guido d'Arezzo revolutionized music by inventing the scale.

Opposite the abbey stands the Palazzo della Ragione where the abbot legislated and administered justice. As a building, it offers a rare example of 11th-century civic architecture, dour yet not without charm.

A miniature Venice, Comacchio lives reflected in lagoon waters.

Inland Excursions

Ferrara

A half-hour drive from the coast lies the sturdy old city of Ferrara, which vied with Venice, Milan and Florence for preeminence in the 15th century.

Ferrara was the citadel of the House of Este, a family as cruel as it was creative. If the Estes devoted much time and energy to intrigues and murder plots against one another, they were also superbly generous in their patronage of the arts and letters. A university was founded in the city in the 14th century, whose library contains the manuscript of *Orlando Furioso,* published in 1516, the great best-seller of the day. Written by Ludovico Ariosto (1474–1533), it dealt with the tribulations of the knight Roland, who was madly infatuated with the temptress Angelica. Ariosto wrote the work while in the diplomatic service of Cardinal Ippolito d'Este, son of Duke Ercole 1. This, too, was the home-town of the religious reformer Girolamo Savonarola (1452–98).

Ferrara enjoyed its golden age—an enormous building spree that crushed the poor tax-payer—under Ercole I. He laid out spacious new quarters, according to plans by Biagio Rossetti, making it the first "modern" city in Europe. Then, in 1598, Ferrara came under the control of the Papal States and a slow decline set in. But it remains an impressive city today, with numerous pedestrian malls and shopping areas closed off to traffic.

In the centre of the old walled town stands the **Castello Estense,** a superb example of medieval architecture. A wide water-filled moat, spanned by drawbridges, surrounds the castle, and its graceful courtyard is framed by four massive corner-towers. Inside, you can tour the history-steeped rooms, including a cell where the wife and step-son of Niccolò III, accused of adultery, were imprisoned before being beheaded.

Connected to the castle by a bridge is the **Palazzo Comunale,** or town hall, once the residence of the Este dukes. The 13th-century palace boasts a handsome staircase in the courtyard by Benvenuti (1481).

Ferrara's **cathedral,** facing

Ferrara's moated medieval castle defies time—and anything else.

the palace, is named after St. George. Its impressive marble façade with three arcaded bays successfully blends the Lombard version of Romanesque with Gothic. Along one flank, you'll see the loggia built in 1472 for a market and shops. The imposing campanile, probably designed by Alberti, was added during the Renaissance.

It's worth visiting the cathedral's **museum** for two impressive paintings by Cosmè Tura, the *Annunciation* and *St. George Slaying the Dragon;* the *Madonna of the Pomegranate* and other sculptures by Jacopo della Quercia; and some fine 12th-century marble bas-reliefs depicting the 12 months.

On Corso Ercole I° d'Este, about 500 yards north of the castello, is one of the most famous Este residences, the **Palazzo dei Diamanti,** so-called because of the diamond-shaped pieces of marble —12,000 of them—that cover two sides of the building. Diamonds were the family emblem. Inside, you'll find the **Pinacoteca Comunale,** featuring works by painters of the Ferrara school, notably Ercole de Roberti, Cosmè Tura, Dosso Dossi, Francesco del Cossa, Lorenzo Costa and Garofalo. **54** The latter, the "Raphael of

Ferrara", was a pupil of the great Urbino master.

South-east now of the cathedral, on Via Savonarola, the **Casa Romei** belonged to Giovanni Romei, who was married to an Este princess. The house is adorned with delightful frescoes.

Also in the vicinity, on Corso della Giovecca, the **Palazzina di Marfisa** was the scene of a lively literary salon. One frequent guest was Torquato Tasso (1544–95), who wrote the epic poem *Gerusalemme Liberata* (Jerusalem Liberated) —after *Orlando Furioso,* the most popular book of the 16th and 17th centuries. The house has valuable period furniture, a garden and Marfisa's theatre, where concerts were held.

Perhaps the greatest artistic legacy of the Este family are the beautiful princely palaces of the 15th and 16th centuries. One of the best, the **Palazzo Schifanoia,** houses the Municipal Museum in what were formerly bedrooms and sitting rooms (closed Tuesdays). The Hall of the Months is decorated with some of the best-known Renaissance frescoes on a non-religious theme, the work of Francesco del Cossa and Ercole de Roberti of the Ferrara school.

In the south-east corner of

the walled city, you'll see the stunning **Palazzo di Ludovico il Moro,** built by Rossetti for Ludovico Sforza, the Duke of Milan and husband of Beatrice d'Este. The palace, with its classic arcaded courtyard, now contains the **Museo Archeologico Nazionale,** showcase for the Etruscan and Greek pottery unearthed at Spina (see p. 50).

Bologna

About an hour and a half from Ravenna lies Bologna, capital of Emilia-Romagna, a vigorous city and the gastronomic high temple of Italy. The handsome old town, built mostly of brick, has a marvellous civic centre and blocks of distinctive arcaded streets.

Etruscan in origin, Bologna (called Felsina at the time) occupied a strategic site between the Po Valley and peninsular Italy. It became a municipality of the Roman Empire in 189 B.C. (they called it Bononia). The famous Bologna school of law, probably founded in the 5th century, developed in the 11th century into a university and ranks as Europe's oldest; its reputation for law and theology in the Middle Ages was proverbial. Here, too, the oldest philharmonic academy was founded by Vincenzo Car-

First Family

It all started with Alberto Azzo II (996–1097), who was invested with the fief of Este. It lasted until 1803 with the death of Ercole III Rinaldo.

Among the most illustrious members of the family:

Niccolò III (1393–1441), a wise and resourceful ruler who extended his domain to include Ferrara, Modena, Parma, Reggio and Milan. He is also credited with doing away with his wife and her lover, and with engendering two cultivated and capable sons, Leonello and **Borso.** Borso added Duke of Ferrara to the family titles.

The very intelligent **Ercole I** (1431–1505) married Eleanor of Aragon, no mean politician herself. In Ercole's absence, she foiled a plot by his nephew to take over, had the traitor beheaded and wept dutifully at the funeral.

Ercole's two beautiful daughters, **Beatrice d'Este**, Duchess of Milan, and **Isabella d'Este,** Marchesa of Mantua, upheld the family name as patrons of arts and letters and foxy diplomats.

Alfonso I (1486–1534) was the military talent. But he is better known as the third husband of the infamous and beguiling Lucrezia Borgia— perhaps his greatest strategic victory.

racci in 1666; Mozart came and passed his exams in 1770, and obtained his musical diploma.

Bologna emerged as a free commune in the 12th century. Later it was the scene of hard-fought struggles between noble families (Pepoli, Visconti, Bentivoglio) and popes. Once Pope Julius II had finally incorporated the city into the Papal States in 1506, Bologna enjoyed three centuries of peace.

Towards the end of World War II, the city served as the pivot of the German defence line and was not liberated until April 21, 1945. Since then, the city has gained attention as the first major Italian municipality to have a Communist administration.

Among Bologna's noted native sons are six popes, plus an impressive smattering of famous artists, including Correggio, the three Carracci, Domenichino, Guido Reni, Il Guercino and Albani. Composer Ottorino Respighi was born here, as well as the great inventor Guglielmo Marconi and the physicist Luigi Galvani.

Let's start sightseeing at the very heart of the town, the superb civic ensemble of Piazza Maggiore and Piazza

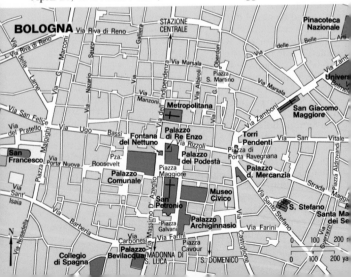

del Nettuno. Pleasant sidewalk cafés line the arcaded **Piazza Maggiore**—a splendid vantage point for observing the Bolognese and their city. On the west side lies the mammoth **Palazzo Comunale** (part of which is known as *d'Accursio*), the town hall, made up of several distinct structures from the 13th–15th centuries. The façade has a large Renaissance portal by Galeazzo Alessi, topped by a bronze statue of Pope Gregory XIII, the Bolognese who reformed the calendar. Above, to the left, stands a beautiful terracotta Madonna by Nicolò dell'Arca (1478).

The mayor's office in the town hall overlooks the **Fontana del Nettuno** (Neptune's Fountain) the famous symbol of the city, designed by Tommaso Laureti. The massive bronze figure with trident, known as *il Gigante* (1566), is the work of Jean de Boulogne, a Frenchman who became one of Italy's leading sculptors under the name of Giovanni da Bologna or Giambologna.

On the other side of the Piazza del Nettuno is the Gothic **Palazzo di Re Enzo,** named after the hapless king of Sardinia, son of Emperor Frederick II, who was held prisoner here for more than 20 years until his death in 1272.

The adjoining **Palazzo del Podestà** (13th century) is notable for its tower, Torre dell'Arengo, which has an archway running through it. Terracotta statues of the city's patron saints adorn the building's corners.

Across the piazza, the enormous basilica of **San Petronio** was begun in 1390—but never finished—on the basis of plans by Antonio di Vincenzo. Notice the very fine Gothic brickwork façade. The central **doorway** is a masterpiece by Jacopo della Quercia: overhead, a bas-relief of the Virgin and Child with Sts. Petronius and Ambrose, and along the side, figures from the Bible. Around the basilica's vast interior are chapels decorated with frescoes, paintings, stained-glass windows and sculptures. In 1530, Charles V was crowned Holy Roman Emperor here by Pope Clement VII.

Next door is the **Museo Civico,** with a rare collection of Etruscan works from the Bologna area, plus many other Roman, Greek and Egyptian antiquities.

The university has found other quarters today, but in the 16th century it was lodged in the **Palazzo Archiginnasio,** just across the street from the Museo Civico. Presently used as the communal library, its walls are decorated with the coats-of-arms of former rectors and professors. In the same building, you can visit the historic Teatro Anatomico, with two remarkable wooden anatomical figures.

The **Palazzo Bevilacqua,** some 300 yards down Via D'Azeglio from Piazza Maggiore, is the best example of Florentine Renaissance in Bologna. The Council of Trent found shelter here briefly in 1547 when Trento was ravaged by an epidemic.

Another ancient university building (just behind Palazzo Bevilacqua) is the **Collegio di Spagna,** founded in 1365 for Spanish students. Ignatius Loyola, founder of the Jesuit Order, and Cervantes were among the boarders.

Back on Piazza Maggiore, follow Via Rizzoli to **Piazza di Porta Ravegnana.** During the 12th and 13th centuries, some 200 towers were erected in Bologna by the commune and by local notables. Two of them, the Torri Pendenti, still stand on this piazza and have become city landmarks. You'll notice that they are both askew: the tall one, **Torre degli Asinelli,** leans about 3½ feet off centre and provides a fine view from on high; the shorter

one, **Torre Garisenda,** which tilts 10 feet in the other direction, figures in Dante's *Inferno.*

Just south of the Torri Pendenti is the elegant **Palazzo della Mercanzia.** This Gothic structure of 1382–84, once the meeting place of the Bolognese merchants, now, appropriately, houses the local chamber of commerce.

A few blocks to the south on Via Santo Stefano, you'll find the fascinating **Santo Stefano,** actually a complex of

churches, mostly Romanesque. The oldest, Santi Vitale e Agricola, was founded perhaps as early as the 5th century, but it has many later additions including three apses from the 11th century. Santissimo Crocefisso has a crypt from 1019 under a 17th-century choir. You pass through the polygonal Santo Sepolcro to get to Cortile di Pilato, a courtyard which takes its name from an ancient basin supposedly used by Pontius Pilate. The carvings on the marble columns of the cloister are said to have inspired Dante in his description of punishments in the *Inferno*. Chiesa della Trinità was built in the early 13th century.

Among other churches scattered through Bologna, don't overlook **San Giacomo Maggiore** (Via Zamboni, just north of Torri Pendenti). It's worth

Bologna's Duomo has seen many historic events in its 500 years.

visiting for the chapel of the powerful Bentivoglio family, with an altarpiece by Francia and frescoes by Lorenzo Costa, and for the Oratorio di Santa Cecilia, which also has fine frescoes by these two artists. The famed friar St. Dominic is buried in **San Domenico** (Via Garibaldi, two blocks south of Palazzo Archiginnasio), built in the 13th century and redone in the baroque period. Nicola Pisano, Nicolò dell'Arca and Michelangelo all had a hand in the decoration of the saint's tomb. **San Francesco** (Piazza San Francesco, west of Piazza Maggiore), a Gothic basilica, is adorned with a stunning marble altar, the work of Pier Paolo dalle Masegne. In the eastern quarter (Strada Maggiore), **Santa Maria dei Servi** deserves a look for its graceful portico and for Cimabue's *Madonna* within. Bologna's cathedral, **Metropolitana** (or San Pietro —Via dell'Indipendenza), has ancient origins but a baroque reworking. The highlight inside is the *Annunciation* by Ludovico Carracci.

In addition to the Museo Civico (p. 57), any visitor's museum list should include the **Pinacoteca Nazionale,** Via delle Belle Arti, 56. This national picture gallery concentrates on the Bolognese school from the 14th to 18th centuries. The Carracci, Il Guercino, Reni, Albani, G. M. Crespi, Gandolfi, Francesco Francia are among the most important. But don't miss Vitale da Bologna's *St. George and the Dragon,* Francesco del Cossa's *Madonna Enthroned* and the fine works by Ercole de Roberti, from Ferrara. There is also a notable collection of Italian masters who worked in Bologna—like Giotto, Perugino and Raphael. The latter is represented by his monumental *Ecstasy of St. Cecilia.*

From the **Madonna di San Luca** on Guardia hill, you have a superb view of Bologna and the Apennines. To get there, you should take a taxi or climb up to the church by following an arcade with 666 arches from the Porta Saragozza. The sanctuary, which was rebuilt in the 18th century by Dotti, takes its name from the 12th-century Byzantine-style painting in the chancel.

While in Bologna, known within Italy as "Bologna la Grassa" or Bologna the Fat,

Muted roofscape of Bologna, the prosperous gastronomic capital.

you must sample the world-renowned cuisine. Almost any restaurant will do. Bolognese specialities include pasta—especially *tortellini*, meat sauce, *mortadella* (Bologna sausage), and *zampone* (stuffed pig's trotters) which often appear in a *bollito misto*, a mixture of boiled meat and sausages.

Veneto to Trieste

Po River Delta

At the Po Delta, you arrive in the Veneto, one of Italy's most varied and popular regions. The lower Veneto near the Adriatic is level, marked by lagoons and *lidi*, where the sediment from the Alpine riv-

ers has been deposited. It is a misty, marshy place with enormous horizons. Away from the sea, at the foothills of the Alps, you'll find bracing air, many villas and beautiful vineyards that produce some of the country's best-known wines. Higher up, the mountains stretch from the Lake of Garda to the Austrian border. It's a region rich in history, natural beauty and works of art.

Spreading out into the Adriatic lies the great Po River Delta *(Polesine)*, with its many mouths. This is haunting and unspoiled country, covered by a great bowl of sky. The virgin shores are planted with juniper and tamarisk, the air is redolent with the resin of the umbrella pines. In the vast flat fields and marshes, women work the crops, while the men pole the fishing barges. At sunset, the *bragozzi*, two-masted boats, return along the *ghebbi*, the small lagoon channels, with the day's catch.

The tidal sea creates salty ponds rich in mullet, bass, sole, plaice, and eel—ideal for sport fishermen. The delta is also famed for its duck shoots. Much of the area has been given national park status, so check with the tourist office about the fishing and hunting regulations. It's possible to take an excursion by boat through the delta.

A few miles from the mouth of the Po lies the ancient town of ADRIA—the city that gave its name to the Adriatic Sea. It was an important Etruscan harbour, known to the Greeks and Romans as Hatria or Atria. The silting of the Po and Adige rivers gradually moved the shoreline eastwards, and with it the importance of Adria declined.

Today, it is a small, undistinguished town, but the **Museo Archeologico** bears witness to Adria's more illustrious past with Etruscan, Greek and Roman artefacts found in the area. Of special interest is the 4th-century B.C. iron chariot of a Gaulish warrior, discovered with the horses' skeletons. The church of Santa Maria Assunta contains a baptismal font from the 8th century.

Between the Po Delta and the Venetian Lagoon lies the newly developed resort complex of ROSOLINA MARE, popular because of its 5-mile strip of sandy beach backed up by vast pine groves. Here you'll find modern hotels, tourist villages and campsites. The beaches are gentle, ideal for children, and for those looking for it, there's lots of nightlife.

At the southern end of the

Venetian Lagoon, you'll see another rapidly expanding beach complex centering around Sottomarina and Chioggia.

Like Venice, **Chioggia** is built on islands with connecting bridges over the canals. One of the main fishing ports of Italy, this town of pre-Roman origin has distinctive pastel-coloured houses with red-tile roofs. It's pleasant to explore the alleys and piazzas on foot. You'll know the Piazzetta Vigo by its column bearing the Lion of St. Mark. Across the bridge, the church of **San Domenico** contains a painting of St. Paul by Carpaccio and a Crucifixion attributed to Tintoretto. The town's cathedral, redone by Longhena after a fire in 1623, is richly decorated in marble.

While in Chioggia, be sure to visit the **fish markets,** and by all means sample the delicious local catch. You can make an entire meal of seafood, whether fish soup, cold seafood salad, risotto with squid, spaghetti with clam sauce, mixed fish fry, sautéed shrimp, lagoon-bred eel prepared in a lemon, oil and tuna sauce.

SOTTOMARINA boasts a wide powdery beach which serves as Chioggia's *lido.* It has plenty of bathing and sports facilities and good accommodation.

Padua *(Padova)*

North-west of Chioggia near the Brenta River lies the wonderful old city of Padua, the adopted home of St. Anthony. According to legend, Padua was founded by Antenor, the Trojan prince. Inhabited by the Veneti tribe, it became one of the most important and wealthy cities in the Roman Empire. In the 14th century, Padua was ruled by the Carraresi family until its conquest in 1405 by Venice.

The **University of Padua,** founded in 1222, attracted students from all over Europe. Known as *il Bo,* The Ox, for the inn which once occupied the site, it is still the most important university scholastically in Italy. It earned Padua the title of *la Dotta,* The Learned.

You can visit the anatomy theatre, built in 1594, the first of its kind on the Continent. The Great Hall, covered with old student coats-of-arms, has the rostrum from which Galileo gave his lectures in physics between 1592 and 1610. One of his pupils was the (future) King Gustavus Adolphus of Sweden. Other famous personalities who attended the university included Dante and Petrarch.

Today, Padua is a remarkably human city with graceful

BERLITZ® GOES VIDEO – *FOR LANGUAGES*

Here's a brand new 90-minute video from Berlitz for learning key words and phrases for your trip. It's easy and fun. Berlitz language video combines computer graphics with live action and freeze frames. You see on your own TV screen the type of dialogue you will encounter abroad. You practice conversation by responding to questions put to you in the privacy of your own living room.

Shot on location for accuracy and realism, Berlitz gently leads you through travel situations towards language proficiency. Available from video stores and selected bookstores and Berlitz Language Centers everywhere. Only $59.95 plus $3.00 for shipping and handling.

To order by credit card, call 1-800-228-2028 Ext. 35.
Coming soon to the U.K.

BERLITZ®
GUIDES

BERLITZ® GOES VIDEO – *FOR TRAVEL*

Travel Tips from Berlitz – now an invaluable part of the informative and colourful videocassette series of more than 50 popular destinations produced by Travelview International. Ideal for planning a trip or as a souvenir of your visit, Travelview videos provide 40 to 60 minutes of valuable information including a destination briefing, a Reference Guide to local hotels and tourist attractions plus practical Travel Tips from Berlitz.

Available from leading travel agencies and video stores everywhere in the U.S.A. and Canada or call 1-800-325-3108 (Texas, call (713) 975-7077; 1-800 661 9269 in Canada). Coming soon to the U.K.

Travelview
INTERNATIONAL
5630 Beverly Hill
Houston, Texas 77057

Among incomparable treasures in Padua is Giotto's Kiss of Judas.

arcades, piazzas bustling with people, and even the casual visitor experiences a distinct sense of civic cohesion and community.

In the centre of the old city, you'll be awed by the **Palazzo della Ragione,** built in 1218–19 as a community council hall. Inside *il Salone,* as it's commonly known, a vast 260-foot long hall contains a heroic wooden horse inspired by Donatello's *Gattamelata* statue (see below).

The Ragione stands hedged between two picturesque squares: Piazza delle Erbe and Piazza della Frutta, the vegetable and fruit markets. Via San Clemente leads to Piazza dei Signori where the Venetian emissaries lived. On the square, you'll see the column of the winged Lion of St. Mark, the marble Loggia della Gran Guardia, an elegant Renaissance structure, and the Palazzo del Capitanio with an enormous 15th-century astronomical clock over the archway.

The **Basilica di Sant'Antonio,** which contains St. Anthony's relics, is one of the most revered shrines in Italy. With a Romanesque façade and **65**

Gothic interior, the imposing church, crowned by eight Byzantine cupolas plus little bell towers and spires, looks rather like a mosque with minarets. Construction of *il Santo*, as it's called, began in 1232, soon after the death and canonization of St. Anthony. He had come from Lisbon as a missionary and landed up in Padua after a storm in the Adriatic. He spent the rest of his life there, where his sermons inspired enthusiasm, and where he was revered.

The main altar of the church is decorated with the celebrated **bronze sculptures** of Donatello. And in the square outside you will find Donatello's superb bronze equestrian statue of **Gattamelata,** the *condottiero* who fought for Venice (1370–1443).

Also on the Piazza del Santo are the **Scuola del Santo** (School of the Saint) with paintings of the life of St. Anthony (two are by Titian), and the **Museo Civico,** which has works by Giotto, Giovanni Bellini, Giorgione, Titian, Veronese, Tiepolo and other "greats".

Not far away, on Prato della Valle—a large piazza surrounded by a canal that reflects the statues of some 80 famous men—is the Santo's

look-alike, **Santa Giustina.** It, too, is decked with eight Byzantine cupolas but is a much later, 16th-century, construction. The altarpiece, the *Martyrdom of St. Justina,* is by Veronese.

In the northern part of the old city near the walls you will find Padua's jewel, the **Cappella degli Scrovegni.** Built in 1305, the chapel shelters a brilliant series of frescoes by Giotto, recounting the lives of Mary and Jesus. The figures are sharply modelled, their gestures remarkably vigorous. Two of the best-known scenes are the *Kiss of Judas* and the *Entombment.* Altogether they show Giotto at his finest.

Almost next door to the Scrovegni, the church of Eremitani is worth visiting for its splendid **Cappella Ovetari,** adorned with frescoes by Andrea Mantegna. The paintings, partly destroyed by Allied bombing in World War II, deal with St. James and St. Christopher. They were done by Mantegna when he was just 18.

You shouldn't leave Padua without visiting the famous

Padua's basilica houses the tomb of St. Anthony, its patron saint.

Caffè Pedrocchi, designed by Giuseppe Japelli in 1831. This elegant, neo-classical building is associated with the patriots of the Risorgimento, who came here regularly along with artists, writers and scholars. You can sit on the patio, sip your drink and feel the rhythm of Padua as its people stream by.

Around Padua

There's no shortage of interesting excursions to make in the area around Padua. To the south-west, the **Euganean Hills,** of volcanic origin, offer lovely landscapes and thermal springs. The wine produced here is sold under the name of Colli Euganei. You can circle the hills in a few hours by car,

Villages—and faces—mellowed by the sun and time. Arquà Petrarca where Petrarch died typifies the hill country round Padua, full of memories.

visiting the spas and charming old towns.

The main spas are **Abano Terme** and its twin MONTE-GROTTO TERME, both popular since Roman times, and BATTAGLIA TERME. The first two are known both for their hot springs and the mud formed by the mineralization of the abundant algae—supposedly very beneficial in the treatment of rhumatism and arthritis. Battaglia Terme was a favourite of literary figures like Heinrich Heine and Stendhal.

Local points of interest include the Benedictine monastery of PRAGLIA founded in 1080, though most of the present buildings are Renaissance. EREMO DI RUA is a hermitage run by the Camaldulian order. Women aren't admitted, but in any case the real reason for going there is the fantastic **panorama**—from Padua all the way to Venice. VALSANZIBIO has the lovely **Villa Barbarigo** (Pizzoni-Ardemagni), a 17th-century estate with magnificent gardens and a maze.

The medieval town of **Arquà Petrarca** was the final home (1370–74) of the great humanist and poet, Petrarch. His house, including the chair he died in, remains a memorial. He is buried in a pink-marble

tomb in front of the local church. To the south, **Monselice** lies at the foot of a hill that is topped by one of Frederick II's fortresses. A good part of the old walls still stand. There are also some fine villas, a 13th-century castle with a museum, a Romanesque-Gothic cathedral and the harmonious Piazza Manzini.

A few miles west is **Este,** the ancient Ateste, an important centre of the Veneti tribe. It is also the ancestral home of **69** the powerful Este family who dominated the region as dukes of Ferrara. You'll find the ruins of a huge medieval castle, complete with crenellated walls, and a cathedral containing a fine Tiepolo. The **Museo Nazionale Atestino,** installed in a 16th-century palace, is noted for its outstanding pre-Roman and Roman collections.

Scattered all over the Veneto are impressive stately homes known as the **Venetian villas.** Nearly 2,000 of them were built by wealthy nobles of the Venetian republic between the 15th and 18th centuries. Dozens of the villas are visitable—and eminently worth visiting. You can either organize your own itinerary or take a tour from Padua or Vicenza.

The highest concentration of Venetian villas can be found along the Brenta Canal between Padua and Venice. A tourist boat, a modern version of the 17th-century *burchiello,* makes the trip lasting eight hours several times a week in season, or you can drive along the canal. At sunset, with the light playing over the ochre buildings, it's not hard to imagine 18th-century Venetians strolling on the lawns listening to the music of Vivaldi.

Heading east from Padua, you come first to the imposing **Villa Nazionale** (or Pisani) at STRA. A vast park surrounds the house with gardens and a long reflecting pool. Inside are frescoes by Tiepolo. Napoleon bought the estate in 1807 and presented it to his stepson Eugène Beauharnais. Other notable villas along the canal are La Soranza at FIESSO D'ARTICO; the Villa Vernier at MIRA VECCHIA; Palazzo Foscarini at MIRA, where Byron stayed; the recently restored Barchessa Valmarana; and the stately Villa Foscari (1574) by the great Renaissance master Andrea Palladio. It was called *la Malcontenta,* because the owner banished his wife there, making her—understandably—somewhat malcontent.

Three other outstanding villas by Palladio are in the region: the Villa Badoer (1570), 16 kilometres from ROVIGO; the celebrated **Villa Barbaro,** or Volpi (1560–68), at MASER, with marvellous frescoes by Veronese; and on a hilltop near VICENZA, the most famous of all, **La Rotonda.** Finished by Scamozzi after Palladio's death, the villa consists of a domed circular core within a cube. Four Ionic colonnades with wide stairways complete the symmetry.

Venice *(Venezia)*

At the end of the Brenta Canal lies the Venetian Lagoon and Venice, the queen of Italy's Adriatic coast. To do justice to this enchanted and enchanting city, a complete guide is required; these few pages can only touch on the highlights*.

The spiritual and geographical centre of Venice is **Piazza San Marco,** a superb architectural ensemble dominated by the **Basilica di San Marco.** Like Venice itself, the basilica is a brilliant compound of East and West, a mixture of styles and constructions that somehow gives you an impression of unity.

The façade is all arches and loggias surmounted by short pointed spires and five sturdy cupolas—each of different dimensions. Until recently, the **quadriga,** four bronze horses with a long and extraordinarily well-travelled history, stood abreast over the main portal. Deterioration by pollution has forced their removal, but replicas fill in for the originals, on view inside. A luminous tapestry of religious **mosaics,** the earliest dating back about 800 years, covers the interior of the basilica. Don't miss **Pala d'Oro,** the shimmering, jewel-encrusted backdrop to the church's main altar.

Outside, the famous **Campanile** is an exact duplicate of the 1,000-year-old bell tower which collapsed in 1902. Take the lift to the top for an unsurpassed **view** of Venice and the lagoon.

Napoleon once called the piazza "Europe's drawing room", and indeed it has a very sociable feeling. People stroll about chatting casually or sit at the outdoor cafés taking in the whole scene. In the background floats the music, romantic and sentimental, of various elegantly attired café orchestras.

Across from the campanile is the graceful **Torre dell'Orologio** (clock tower), where two bronze Moors have been hammering away the hours on the huge bell for almost 500 years —to the delight of the tourists below. The harmonious arcaded piazza is completed by the **Procuratie Vecchie,** originally the residence of the procurators (governor or financial administrator of a minor province), the **Procuratie Nuove,** now a museum, and Ala Napoleonica (Napoleon's wing), with another museum devoted to Venice.

---

* For a stay of more than a day or so, the Berlitz travel guide VENICE gives all the necessary extra information.

71

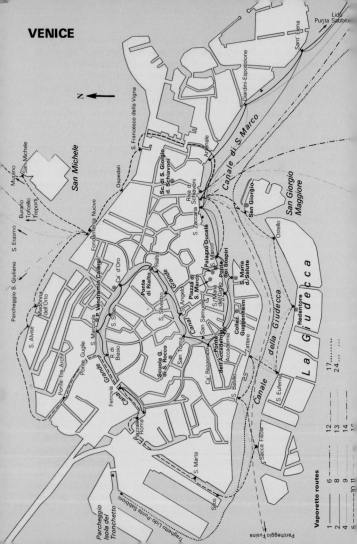

VENICE

N

Lido
Punta Sabbio...

Sant' Elena

San Michele

San Michele

Murano

Burano
Torcello
Treporti

S. Erasmo

S. Giuliano

Parcheggio S. Giuliano

Madonna
dell'Orto

S. Alvisè

Ponte Guglie

R. di
Biasio

Ponte Tre Archi

Ferrovia

Piazzale
Roma

S. Marta

Slps

Parcheggio Lido-Punta Sabbioni

Parcheggio
Isola del
Tronchetto

S. Francesco della Vigna

Ospedali

Fondamenta Nuove

Ca' d'Oro

S. Stae

S. Marcuola

P. Vendramin Calergi

Ponte
di Rialto

Rialto

S. Silvestro

Canal Grande

S. Tomà

San Samuele

San Stae

Scuola G.
di S. Rocco

Ca. Rezzonico

Ponte
dell'Accademia

Accademia

Zattere

S. Basilio

Sc. di S. Giorgio.
d. Schiavoni

Arsenale

Rio d.
Schiavoni

Rivo d.
Schiavoni

S. Zaccaria

Piazza di
S. Marco

S. Maria
del Giglio

S. Maria

Collez.
Guggenheim

S. Eufemia

Giardini-Esposizione

Canale di S. Marco

San Giorgio

San Giorgio
Maggiore

Palazzo Ducale

S. Marco

Ponte
dei Sospiri

S. Maria
d.Salute

Ostello

Redentore

L a   G i u d e c c a

C a n a l e   d e l l a   G i u d e c c a

Sacca Fisola

Fragetto Lido-Punta Sabbioni

Parcheggio Fusina

Vaporetto routes

1	— — —	6 · · · · · · 12 — · — · —
2	— · · —	9 — · — · 13 · · ·
4	— — —	— 14 · — ·
5	10 11	16
		17 · · · · · · · ·
		24 · · ·

Leading off the piazza—and almost a continuation of it—is the **Piazzetta di San Marco.** Two giant granite columns mark its gateway to the sea, one bearing the winged Lion of St. Mark, the other St. Theodore, Venice's first patron saint. On the right side of the piazzetta, you'll see the columned façade of Sansovino's 16th-century **Libreria** (library). The architect had to clear away the public toilets to build his masterpiece.

On the other side is the fabulous **Palazzo Ducale** (Doges' Palace), the seat of Venetian power for 900 years. With its double row of elaborate Gothic arches and its pink and white design, the building is unique. You can visit the palace on your own or take one of the guided tours. The grandiose **Sala del Maggior Consiglio** (Great Council Chamber) is where the citizens of Venice assembled to elect doges and discuss state affairs. Later only the nobles convened here. One whole wall is covered by Tintoretto's *Paradiso,* said to be the largest oil painting in the world. The famous **Ponte dei Sospiri** (Bridge of Sighs) connects the palace to the prisons.

In Venice, you'll undoubtedly make several trips along the **Canal Grande** (Grand Canal), the city's watery main street. You can travel on a *vaporetto* (the equivalent of a bus), a *motoscafo* (speed boat) or a gondola, always expensive —but then what isn't, alas, in this most extravagant of cities? It's possible, though, to sample the joys of a gondola ride, very briefly and cheaply, by taking one of the *traghetti,* the cross-canal gondola ferries.

Starting from the San Marco end of the canal, on the left you have Longhena's magnificent baroque church, **Santa Maria della Salute,** built after a terrible plague in 1630. On the right are some of the city's smartest hotels, like the fabled Gritti Palace. The boat goes under the wooden **Ponte dell'Accademia,** which leads to the **Gallerie dell'Accademia** with its unsurpassed collection of Venetian painters—Veronese, Tintoretto, Titian, Gentile and Giovanni Bellini, Carpaccio, Tiepolo and Giorgione.

Halfway along the two-mile canal are the pleasant embankments of the **Rialto,** one of the few places where you can stroll along the waterway. The area has long been a financial and shopping centre. The **Ponte di Rialto** (Rialto Bridge), with its characteristic hump and a double row of shops, was erected nearly **73**

400 years ago by Antonio da Ponte, winner of a competition for a new bridge that would last.

Along the canal, you'll glide by some 200 palaces—Byzantine and Gothic, Lombard and Renaissance, baroque and classical. The celebrated **Ca' d'Oro,** designed by Longhena, has been imitated everywhere. In the **Palazzo Vendramin Calergi,** a beautiful Lombard-style building, Wagner died in 1883.

The Grand Canal winds past the Ghetto area, the old Jewish quarter, and ends near the Piazzale Roma, where you debark for the car parks.

Among the many churches and monuments of extraordinary artistic merit in Venice are the **Scuola Grande di San Rocco,** with a breathtaking collection of Tintorettos; the **Scuola di San Giorgio degli Schiavoni,** with rare Carpaccio paintings and **Santa Maria Gloriosa dei Frari,** which contains Titian's tomb and two of his finest works, *Assumption* and *Madonna.*

Other churches worth visiting include the Madonna dell'Orto, which has some very good Tintorettos; the exquisite Santa Maria dei Miracoli, the church Venetians prefer to marry in; San Sebastiano,

filled with the painting of Veronese; Santi Giovanni e Paolo, where you can see Giovanni Bellini's polyptych and, in the square outside, that matchless **equestrian statue** of Bartolomeo Colleoni, executed by Andrea Verrocchio in the 15th century.

One of Europe's best collections of modern art is to be found in Peggy Guggenheim's **Palazzo Venier,** now run as a museum by the Guggenheim Foundation of New York (closed in winter).

Just across from Piazzetta di San Marco lies the island of **San Giorgio Maggiore** with its beautiful church by Palladio. From the top of the campanile, you'll find the best view of Venice. On the neighbouring isle of Giudecca is another Palladio masterwork, the Redentore, a church notable for its cool, graceful interior.

The Venetian Lagoon holds many delights for visitors. You can reach the main points of interest by *vaporetto* or on an organized tour. First stop is bound to be the island of **Murano** and its glass-blowing factories. Murano's glass museum contains beautiful specimens dating back five centuries. But don't overlook the little church known as San Donato, founded in the early Romanesque period. It boasts a magnificent mosaic floor and a golden mosaic of the Madonna.

Further west is the picturesque island of **Burano,** a fishing and lace-making centre, beautifully preserved. The campanile of San Martino has a decided tilt to it, the rainbow-coloured houses on the waterfront a great deal of charm.

Torcello, on the other side of Burano, was once a thriving community of 20,000. Today, all that remains is a small **cathedral** with superb Byzantine mosaics of the Virgin and Child and The Last Judgement. Torcello, by the way, has a fine outdoor restaurant, and many tourists make a point of coming over for lunch.

The Venetian Lagoon is enclosed by long strips of beach known as *litorale.* Closest to Venice proper is the world-renowned **Lido** with a string of luxury hotels along the sandy beach. The municipal casino, open in summer, offers gambling and puts on artistic events. The Lido was the setting for Thomas Mann's *Death in Venice.*

Extravagant, enchanted, elusive Venice, half city and half dream.

Treviso

It's only a short excursion inland to Treviso, and one well worth making; it's one of the loveliest cities in the area. Treviso had its golden age under the Da Camino family in the 13th century, and Venetians took over in 1389. Medieval ramparts encircle the old town with its winding streets and small houses decorated with porticos and frescoes. The town's many canals continue to turn mill wheels.

Piazza dei Signori, bordered on three sides by impressive buildings, is the hub of local activity. The **Palazzo dei Trecento** (c. 1217), with its arcaded loggia added in 1552, has been impressively restored since World War II.

The **Duomo,** with seven cupolas, has an elegant three-nave interior containing a famous *Annunciation* by Titian. Treviso's largest church, the Gothic, red-brick **San Nicolò,** is spacious and full of light. Adorning the colossal pillars are marvellous frescoes of the saints by Tommaso da Modena (c. 1323–79). In the austere church of **San Francesco,** you'll see the tombs of Dante's son, Pietro, and Petrarch's daughter, Francesca.

Treviso's **Museo Civico** contains an interesting archaeological section and a picture gallery devoted to local and Venetian artists, such as Tommaso da Modena, Girolamo da Treviso, Giovanni Bellini, Lorenzo Lotto, Titian and Jacopo Bassano.

Veneto Coast

Italy's north Adriatic coast is marked by great lagoons separated from the sea by sandbars, known as *lidi.* These were formed by the sediment washed down from the Alps by rivers like the Po, Adige, Brenta, Piave and Livenza. After the silt has built up off the river's mouth, strong east-west currents shape it into a long strand parallel to the shore. Gradually, the sandbar rises above the water level, becoming the new shoreline.

The resulting lagoons and their low-lying islands, often submerged at high tide, are rich in fish and wildfowl. Venice's lagoon is the largest, and its Lido has become synonymous with a chic bathing resort. But other *lidi* are also noted for their fine beaches.

East of Venice, the LITO- RALE DEL CAVALLINO, connected to the mainland by road, is a favourite with campers. The beach is free, not too crowded and relatively clean. The LIDO DI IESOLO, a 9-mile stretch of beach between the Venetian Lagoon and the Piave, has become enormously popular with both Italians and northern Europeans. Once the Roman port of Jesulum, Iesolo was a refuge for Venetians after the fall of the Roman Empire. Today, the resort complex includes discos, cinemas, miniature golf, two small boat harbours and a roller-skating rink.

On the other side of the River Piave, the equally attractive resort of ERACLEA MARE has a fine sandy beach bordered by thick pine woods, cottages, campsites, tourist villages, restaurants and other facilities.

The picturesque resort of **Caorle** lies on a strip of land surrounded by canals at the mouth of the Livenza River. For many years, this quiet fishing village was the seat of a bishopric and it still has a red-brick Romanesque cathedral (1048) to show for its more illustrious past. Of particular interest are the Byzantine altar screen of gilded silver and the handsome circular campanile. Many of Caorle's shops have been converted into artisan boutiques to attract the tourists who come for the wide stretch of sand on both sides of the Livenza.

The last beach resort in the Veneto is BIBIONE, set like an island between the sea and a series of fishing lagoons and canals. With its good road connections and long sandy beach, Bibione enjoys considerable popularity.

An inland city of note is **Portogruaro,** which has kept much of its medieval and Renaissance character. You'll find cafés near canals over-draped with willows and palms. Take in the Gothic Palazzo Comunale, the Duomo with a leaning Romanesque bell tower and the fine Museo Nazionale Concordiese, with finds from the nearby Roman military colony, Concordia Sagittaria.

Friuli

On the other side of the Tagliamento River begins the region of Friuli-Venezia Giulia, the north-eastern corner of Italy bordering on Austria and Yugoslavia. Like the Veneto, this beautiful area is characterized by lagoons formed by rivers coursing down to the sea from the Alps. But the countryside is more varied here— both softer and more rugged— with a steep limestone plateau, the Carso, along the eastern frontier.

The hard-working farmers of Friuli produce an abundance of grain, fruit, corn and some of Italy's best wines. And they speak a language all their own—Friulian, a Rhaeto-Romanic dialect that is now undergoing something of a renaissance. The region was badly hit by earthquakes in 1976 and many towns in the upper Friuli still bear the scars.

The first resort you come to, and one of the largest tourist complexes of the Italian Adriatic, is LIGNANO SABBIADORO. Composed of three parts—Pineta, Riviera and Sabbiadoro—it lies on a peninsula of fine golden sand between the sea and the lagoon of Marano. With some 400 hotels and pensions and ample camping grounds, newly constructed yacht basins and marinas, a large thermal spa and good sports facilities, Lignano is well prepared for tourism.

Set on an island, the city of **Grado** to the east could also lay claim to the title of the fastest-growing resort on the Adriatic. But unlike Lignano, Grado has a long history dating back to the days when the residents of Aquileia came here in the 5th century to escape the barbarian hordes.

Grado's two large beaches are justly renowned, and the fine crystalline sand has made the resort an important European centre for a form of therapy using sun-heated sand. Because it is 5 kilometres away from the mainland—a long jetty bridges the lagoon—Grado enjoys extremely pure, dust-free air, and the mild climate gives it a long beach season, from May to October.

In the old section of town, the Duomo, **Sant'Eufemia,** with its baptistry and the church of Santa Maria delle Grazie form a notable 6th-century ensemble. There is a well-preserved mosaic floor and a 14th-century silver altar screen worth looking at in the cathedral. Colourful alleys lead down to the port.

Eleven kilometres inland, you'll discover a gem of Roman and medieval history—**Aquileia.** One of the most important cities in the Roman Empire, Aquileia was founded in 181 B.C. as a frontier fort. It became the regional capital and hub of the road network connecting Rome to central Europe. Augustus made the town his headquarters during his campaign against the Germans and received King Herod here a few years before the birth of Christ. In 452, the town was partially destroyed by Attila's Huns; but, after a period of decline, Aquileia again knew greatness in the

A gentle climate, sparkling air and silvery beaches make the island town of Grado one of the fastest-growing holiday centres on the Adriatic.

Middle Ages as the seat of the powerful patriarchate.

Today, Aquileia is a lovely place to visit—serene and deeply imbued with a feeling of the past. Set among pine, cypress and linden trees, the **Basilica** was first built in the early 4th century but reconstructed in its present form in the 11th century by the Patriarch Poppone. A tall campanile stands next to it. The simple interior is graced by a marvellous **mosaic floor** from the original church that tells the story of Jonah and the Whale. You'll see frescoes of scenes of the life of Christ in the 9th-century crypt. A second crypt, **Cripta degli Scavi,** contains superb Roman and Early Christian mosaics.

Behind the church, a path bordered by cypress, known as the Via Sacra, leads to the excavated old Roman harbour and warehouses on the river. The **Museo Archeologico** displays a good collection of local finds, including Roman sculptures, mosaics, jewellery and

79

glass. There's still a lot in Aquileia that remains to be excavated, but don't miss a visit to the various excavation sites—the market place, forum and Roman houses.

If you have time, you should plan to visit **Udine,** capital of Friuli and one of the most graceful towns in Italy—it's less than an hour from the coast. Udine bears the stamp of Venice, which isn't surprising since it lived under its rule from 1420 to 1797. During World War I, it served as the general headquarters of the Italian Supreme Command, until the Austrians took over in 1917.

The heart of the city is the harmonious **Piazza della Libertà** with its Gothic-Venetian Palazzo del Comune in pink-and-white stone (also known as the Loggia del Lionello after the architect). Opposite you'll see the elegant 16th-century Porticato di San Giovanni, surmounted by a clock tower with Venetian-inspired, bell-ringing Moors.

To reach the castle on the hill above, you pass through the **Arco Bollani** (Bollani Arch) designed by Palladio.

Udine, calm and pretty, wears the imprint of its Venetian heritage.

The **Castello** itself, once the residence of the Venetian governors, houses a municipal museum and a gallery with works by Carpaccio, Canova, Ghirlandaio and Tiepolo.

Tiepolo admirers will be amply rewarded in Udine. His **wall paintings** in the cathedral mark a high point in illusionistic art. The Venetian's famous *Assumption* can be seen in the Oratorio across from the cathedral, and a fine series of biblical frescoes are in the Palazzo Arcivescovile on the Piazza del Patriarcato.

As you explore the town, walk through the arcaded streets to the Piazza Matteotti where the colourful market takes place by a 16th-century fountain by Giovanni da Udine, the town's most celebrated son.

About 25 kilometres to the south-west at PASSARIANO stands the **Villa Manin,** the most spectacular country house in this region. Two semi-circular colonnades frame the approach to the main building. The stunning cream-coloured house, designed by Giovanni Ziborghi, belonged to Ludovico Manin, the last doge of Venice. A touch of historical irony: Napoleon lived here in 1797 while working on the Treaty of Campoformio (today Campoformido, 7 kilometres from Udine), by which the Venetian republic was handed over to the Austrians.

East of Udine lies the Carso, a crevassed limestone plateau, part of the Austro-Hungarian Empire until the end of World War I. Some of the bloodiest battles of the war—like Caporetto in 1917—took place in these uplands.

Returning to the coast at the Gulf of Trieste, the shoreline shifts from broad sandy beaches to rocky inlets studded with fishing hamlets. The water below the cliffs ranges from deep green to blue. The small harbours are well equipped for

boating, with several offering lessons in sailing, canoeing and water-skiing. In the hills behind the sea are some cool underground caves—the **Grotta Gigante,** the largest in the region, stands out for its stalactic formations, and at SLIVIA there's the Grotta delle Torri.

The village of DUINO boasts two castles—ruined Castello Vecchio and a handsome newer one, Castello Nuovo, where the German poet Rilke once stayed. SISTIANA is set on a bay in a natural amphitheatre of woods and attractive villas. Towering above the picturesque little seaside town of GRIGNANO stands **Miramare,** a gingerbread castle built in 1856–60 for the Archduke Maximilian of Austria, later the ill-fated Emperor of Mexico. Magnificent terraced gardens surround the castle, where sound-and-light shows are held in summer months. After Miramare, you pass BARCOLA, Trieste's bathing resort.

Trieste and Beyond

Leading seaport of the north Adriatic, Trieste was a city before the Romans came. It overlooks the gulf that bears its name and is backed by a ridge of hills and the Carso.

For many centuries Trieste was locked in a struggle with Venice for supremacy over the north Adriatic. It came under the protection of Austria in 1382 and, in 1719, was declared a free port. The city prospered as the Hapsburg Empire's principal maritime outlet, flourishing particularly after the opening of the Suez Canal in 1869. But Trieste was also a hotbed of Italian nationalism.

At the end of World War I, the city was occupied by the Italians, led by the writer Gabriele d'Annunzio. After World War II, the Yugoslavs took it, but under the terms of the Treaty of Paris in 1947, Trieste again became a free port, while the territory to the north and the Istrian peninsula went to Yugoslavia. Then in 1954, after a plebiscite, the city rejoined Italy.

Explorer Sir Richard Burton served as British consul in Trieste, where he died in 1890. And the great Irish writer, James Joyce, lived here from 1905 to 1914 and again after the war.

Today, you'll find Trieste clean, sturdy and bustling with traffic. City life centres around the **Piazza dell'Unità d'Italia**

82

Trieste looks back on long history stretching to pre-Roman times.

with its imposing city hall, the government palace and headquarters of the farflung Lloyd Triestino Line. Sit down and relax with a coffee or drink at one of the outdoor cafés on the spacious square.

The piazza opens onto the **waterfront,** where you can meander along the pleasant Riva, or promenade, watching the movement of ships in this major port. At one end of the quay, you'll find the lighthouse, at the other the Canal Grande with a small-boat harbour and the church of Sant'Antonio di Padova. The main passenger-ship terminal is at the Molo dei Bersaglieri. Next to the Molo Pescheria, the fish market, stands, fittingly enough, an aquarium, and further on lies the Museo del Mare, retracing the history of local navigation and shipping.

You'll have a splendid view of the city from the **Basilica di San Giusto.** Founded on the site of a Roman temple in the 5th century, the present structure results from a merger in the 14th century of three adjacent Romanesque churches. A beautiful Gothic rose-window dominates the basilica's façade; some remnants of the original Roman temple can be seen in it. Inside are fine mosaics of the Virgin with Archangels Michael and Gabriel and of Christ with Saints Giusto and Servulus. The third church became the baptistry.

Above the cathedral, the **Castello** was begun by the Venetians in 1470 and finished by the Austrians. It now houses several museums, including one with an excellent collection of antique arms. A lush park extends down the hill from the castle.

Heading back down towards the centre, the **Museo di Storia ed Arte** on Via della Cattedrale, contains prehistoric and Roman artefacts, bronzes, glasses and vases. The museum has a cenotaph dedicated to the famous German archaeologist J.J. Winckelmann; he was murdered by a thief in Trieste in 1768 after showing off gold coins he had dug up.

At the bottom of the hill you come to the Arco di Riccardo, an arch first erected to honour Emperor Augustus but later renamed after the English King Richard I, who was mistakenly thought to have been imprisoned in the city. The Via del Teatro Romano leads to the restored remains of a Roman theatre.

Another cluster of museums, down by the waterfront,

includes the **Museo Revoltella** on Via Diaz, with a respectable collection of modern art.

Last stop on Italy's Adriatic coast should be **Muggia,** a fishing port with a pleasant Venetian aspect. The Gothic Duomo has an interesting cut-stone façade with scalloped arches. In MUGGIA VECCHIA (2 kilometres away) you'll find a 9th- to 11th-century basilica and the ruins of the town that was sacked by the Genoese in the 14th century.

From Trieste, organized excursions run to Yugoslavia, to the Istrian peninsula or deeper into Slovenia. Check with the local travel agents for details.

What to Do

Sports

Sunning and Swimming. First of the list, of course, are the long, wide beaches. Their gentle slopes and calm water make them ideal for children (and adults, too). And if you enjoy being pampered, the seaside clubs offer all the comforts of home—chairs, umbrellas, mats and mattresses and refreshments, plus the company of sociable Italians.

Incidentally, the communities along the Adriatic, well aware of the importance of

Rules of the Beach

Italy's beaches are theoretically open to all without charge. In practice, local governments in resort areas usually give the choice pieces of shoreline to bathing-club concessions which rent out chairs, mattresses, umbrellas and changing rooms.

But these operators must provide access to the "public area" of the beach, the 5 metres between the high-tide mark and the sea. So, if you want to, you can walk through the club and plonk yourself down on those free metres of sand. But it's much easier to find a club you like (most are very reasonable) and take advantage of their facilities.

If you have a car and the time to explore out-of-the-way spots along the coast, you can find some completely undeveloped beaches.

tourism, have waged a vigorous campaign against water pollution. Now, with a few exceptions, the sea here is cleaner than elsewhere in Italy.

During the summer months, the rays glancing off the sea are strong. Make sure to use plenty of sun lotion your first few days out and don't stay exposed too long.

Boating. There are dozens of yacht harbours between Ancona and Trieste, and boating is a popular pastime on the Adriatic. You can hire small sailing boats or motorboats in most major resort areas if you don't bring along your own craft. In some places, there are special sailing schools for foreigners. For additional information on sailing, contact the Federazione Italiana Vela, Porticciolo Duca degli Abruzzi, Genoa; for motorboats, the

Federazione Italiana Moto-
nautica, Via Cappuccio, 19,
Milan.

Windsurfing. Windsurfing
schools have sprung up in Rimini, Cesenatico, Cervia and a
number of other resorts along
the Adriatic. They generally
offer week-long courses for
beginners and advanced prac-
titioners.

Water-skiing. Water-skiing
has an increasing number of
devotees, not only along the
sea but also in the lagoons

and river deltas. You can take
lessons at the bigger spas. For
more details, contact the Federazione Italiana Sci Nautico,
Viale Rimembranze di Greco,
1, Milan.

**Snorkelling and Scuba Div-
ing.** The best stretches of the
Adriatic for underwater exploration are the rocky shore near
Ancona and the coast north-
west of Trieste. Underwater
fishing, free in Italian territo-
rial waters, is prohibited within
500 metres of bathing beaches. **87**

You must indicate your submerged presence by a float on the surface with the appropriate flag. You'll find compressed air and diving equipment at most major resorts.

Fishing. You can fish in the sea from the shore or from a boat without a licence, though some ports require a permit from the harbourmaster. A number of resorts organize charter boats for a day's trolling on the Adriatic.

You do need a licence, issued by the provincial administration, to fish in the rivers and inland lakes. The Federazione Italiana della Pesca, which has branches in each provincial capital, provides information on local regulations.

Hunting. Though the game and bird population has been sadly depleted, hunting is still popular in Italy, particularly in the marshes of the lagoons. Check with tourist authorities for seasonal dates and regulations.

Golf. While not exactly a flourishing sport here, golf courses can be found near the bigger cities and in the newer resorts. There are 18-hole courses at Isola di Albarella-Rosolina, Mogliano Veneto near Treviso, Padua and the Venice Lido; 9-hole courses at Fagagna near Udine, at

Udine, Trieste and Vittorio Veneto north of Treviso.

Tennis. Almost every community in the Adriatic region has tennis courts, clay or hard-surface. Municipal courts can usually be rented for a straight fee, but to play on those belonging to clubs it may be necessary to take out a temporary membership.

Riding. Horseback riding is a traditional sport in Italy, and there are numerous centres where you can spend a holiday, so to speak, on horseback. Many Adriatic resorts have horses to hire by the hour or day. For further details, write to the A.N.T.E. (National Association of Equestrian Tourism), Largo Messico, 13, Rome.

Walking. Hikers will find trails to tramp along in the Apennines and Dolomites. Ask local tourist authorities about regional possibilities.

Skiing. Although most people think of the Adriatic region as a centre for summer sports, some of Italy's best skiing is just a few hours from the coast.

The major ski resorts are concentrated in the Dolomites, but new resorts are now appearing in the Julian Alps of Friuli and the Apennines of central Italy.

Entertainment

Evening activities usually centre around restaurants, outdoor cafés and discotheques. There is one gambling casino in the region, at Venice's Lido (which moves to the Palazzo Vendramin Calergi on the Grand Canal from October to March).

You'll often hear band concerts by a local ensemble in the town's main piazza, but you can also find more serious music, opera and theatrical galas along the Adriatic.

Many cities stage lively folklore festivals, in which the local citizenry don traditional costumes. In the Marches and Romagna, the events tend to run to tournaments—like the crossbow competition at Gradara, or carnivals, like the one in Fano where they parade a

Venice takes on fairytale magic at Carnival and Regatta time.

huge marionette through town. The origin of Fano's procession is lost in history, but the giant figure was constructed in 1883.

Festivals generally involve plenty of eating and drinking. Under the pretext of commemorating a historic event or honouring a local saint, some villages stage fêtes featuring tableloads of free food and wine. Cattolica's fish-fry in June is one of the best.

Further north, in the Veneto and Friuli, there are numerous festivities connected with the sea. In Grado, on the first Sunday of July, a procession of boats bedecked with flags and carrying a statue of the Madonna sails to the island of Barbana, as it has every year since 1237. But the most famous nautical spectacle of all is Venice's Regata Storica held in September, a colourful parade of boats and barges complete with a make-believe doge.

Shopping

Many visitors to Italy consider shopping an important part of the trip. The reputation for quality and style still holds (prices, alas, slightly less), and in the cities and villages of the Adriatic the range is vast —from elegant high fashion creations of Venetian couturiers to simple ceramic dishes produced in the hill towns.

And, in fact, in this area one of the best buys is the local **pottery.** The artisans of Faenza and surrounding villages design brightly coloured, glazed earthenware known as majolica. Pesaro, Fano and Urbino

A little bit of Italy to carry back. These rosy-cheeked dolls are longing to find a real home.

are also noted for their ceramics.

The Adriatic, like all of Italy, sells fine **leather goods.** Superbly styled handbags and shoes cost about the same here as standard articles back home. Similarly, Italian **silks**— scarves, blouses and ties—are tasteful and good value for money, though they, too, can be pricey.

Handsome **hand-printed cloth,** curtains and bedspreads, on which the patterns have been stamped with old wooden moulds in the traditional bright blue and rust colours are a speciality of the area around Forlì.

And don't forget about hand-made **lace.** Lace-making more or less began in Venice, and artisans of Burano and Torcello still produce exquisite table cloths and other items on their small pillows.

Venice itself is renowned for **glassware,** which comes in every imaginable size, shape and colour. Though some of the blown glass tends to be rather garish—green spaniels with red eyes or gold-trimmed purple goblets—there is also some excellent modern design in the better shops, simple, elegant crystal that ranks with the best. And it's always interesting to visit a glass-blowing factory, even if the finished product is not exactly to your taste.

When it comes to **antiques,** here as elsewhere the motto remains: *caveat emptor,* let the buyer beware. While you may find something lovely and not too expensive in an out-of-the-way country place, the chances are that the antique dealers have already been there, and it's not impossible that your discovery is a reproduction. Unless you know the field very well, you will be better off

with a reputable dealer though you'll pay accordingly.

A Paduan, Bartolomeo Cristofori, is credited with inventing the piano, and the city continues the keyboard tradition with the manufacture of organs. Other **musical instruments** made in the Adriatic region include accordions, saxophones and guitars, usually at reasonable prices.

If you're looking for bargains, consider the Italian chain stores like UPIM, Standa, Coin and la Rinascente. And, the local outdoor **markets,** lively and fun to wander through. Items of special interest in markets are wrought-iron work, beaten copper and brassware, baskets and articles of plaited straw.

While major stores stand by their listed prices, you may be able to bargain a little in small shops and especially in the market. Ask the merchant if he will give you a discount *(sconto).*

And, finally, as a souvenir of your visit, what could be better than a fine bottle of local wine or some *grappa,* guaranteed to put you in a holiday mood back home?

Shops are generally open from 8 or 9 a.m. to 12.30 or 1 p.m. and from 3 or 4 to 7 or 8 p.m.

Eating Out

Italians like to eat and to eat well, and the cuisine along the Adriatic is as varied and sophisticated as any in Italy*. The diversity of climate and terrain produces a wide range of high quality ingredients which the local culinary tradition turns into marvellous pasta, rice dishes, sausages, cheese and desserts. And, furthermore, some of the country's best wines come from vineyards located in the foothills behind the Adriatic.

Regions and Restaurants

You'll discover that the provinces of the Marches and Friuli-Venezia Giulia have straightforward, robust fare, rather like the people who live there. In the Marches, specialities include fish soup, roasts and suckling pig, as well as *lasagna*, known locally as *vincisgrassi*. Friuli is noted for its game, *prosciutto* (ham) from San Daniele, spicy *luganica* sausage, *ricotta* cheese and pastries with an Austrian touch.

The Adriatic Riviera belongs to the province of Emilia-Romagna, a region with a reputation for outstanding food. You'll be served pasta in all shapes and sizes, often with the famous meat sauce of Bologna, *ragù*. From Parma comes superb cured ham and parmesan *(parmigiano)* cheese. *Cotechino* and *zampone* (actually a stuffed pig's foot) are traditional pork sausages.

Perhaps the most subtle cooking is to be found in the Veneto. Fish, especially shellfish, reign here, but don't miss the risotto, a luscious rice dish prepared with peas *(risi e bisi)* or shrimp *(con scampi)* for example. The Venetians' most famous meat dish is *fegato alla veneziana*, liver thinly sliced and sautéed with onions. They serve it with polenta (a purée of maize or cornmeal) that turns up on many dishes—grilled, fried, plain or with a sauce.

Italians tend to make a ritual out of eating. If you're bewildered by the elaborate (often hand-written) menu, ask the proprietor or waiter for some recommendations. Many Italians take their main (three-or four-course) meal in the middle of the day, but along the Adriatic, where they're used to the habits of foreigners, it's usually possible to have just a salad or a plate of pasta.

*For a comprehensive glossary of Italian wining and dining, ask your bookshop for the Berlitz EUROPEAN MENU READER.

Of course, for a light meal, you can miss out the *ristorante* or *trattoria* (generally but not always simpler) and look for a *tavola calda*, a cafeteria-style restaurant serving hot dishes at low prices, a pizzeria or a stand-up bar which offers sandwiches and snacks. Some of the finest restaurants in Italy are unpretentious, so don't equate the cuisine with the décor.

All restaurants, no matter how modest, must now issue a formal bill *(ricevuta fiscale)* with VAT, or sales tax *(I. V. A.)*. A customer may actually be stopped outside the premises and fined if he cannot produce this receipt. The bill usually includes cover *(coperto)* and service *(servizio)* charges as well. It's customary to leave about 10% for the waiter.

Lunch normally begins around 1 o'clock, dinner at 8 or 9 p.m., but hotels tend to open their dining rooms earlier for the foreign tourists.

Antipasti and Pasta
In Italy, you generally start off your meal with an antipasto, a bowl of soup *(minestra)*, a dish of pasta or, for robust appetites, some of each. The antipasto might be a plate of cold meat, such as the *mortadella* sausage from Bologna or garlic salami from Ferrara or one of the excellent cured hams like *prosciutto di Parma* or *di San Daniele* (considered by some gourmets to be the best). The ham may be served with melon or figs, a wonderful combination of sweet and salty.

Fish lovers should try the *antipasto* (or *insalata*) *di frutti di mare*, a cold dish of shrimp, crab, squid and other crustaceans marinated in oil and lemon juice, and the *cozze alla marinara*, mussels cooked in white wine with parsley and garlic. In the Veneto, gourmets appreciate the red *granzeole* crabs you eat directly from the shell. And there are various types of fish soup, *brodetto di pesce*, the Italian version of bouillabaisse.

For chilly days, there's *pasta e fagioli*, a hearty soup of noodles and white beans.

In the pasta department, the Adriatic offers a vast selection. In Emilia-Romagna and the Marches, order some *tagliatelle*, thin flat ribbons of egg noodle, *lasagne verdi al forno*, layers of green pasta filled with meat and baked; *cannelloni*, *tortellini*, *cappelletti* and *agnolotti* are ravioli-like pasta in different shapes. If it's described as *magro*, it means the stuffing does not contain meat.

Rice dishes are a favourite

of the northern Adriatic region. Try the *risotto primavera*, cooked with fresh vegetables, *risotto pescatore* with mixed seafood or *risotto con le seppie*, a Venetian speciality made with cuttlefish and its ink.

Main Courses

Seafood, of course, is the star of Adriatic cuisine. *Sogliola* (sole), *calamari* (squid), *branzino* or *spigola* (sea-bass), *triglia* (red mullet), *anguilla* (eel) and *coda di rospo* (literally, "toad's tail"), a mild, firm-fleshed fish, are just a few of the choices you'll see on menus. *Baccalà alla vicentina* is salt cod simmered in milk with anchovy and garlic; *gamberetti*, *gamberi* and *scampi* (shrimps or prawns) may appear boiled, fried or grilled. But if you can't decide among all the tantalizing possibilities, opt for a *fritto misto*, mixed fish fry.

Inland, the taste runs to meat. You'll find beef *(manzo* or *bue)*, lamb *(agnello)*,

pork *(maiale)* and more commonly veal *(vitello)*. *Pollo alla padovana*, chicken spiced and roasted on the spit, comes from Padua; *coniglio* is rabbit.

The region of Emilia-Romagna is known for its pork specialities—*culatello*, highly flavoured ham, *coppa*, cured pork shoulder, and *zampone*. Another Romagna classic, *bollito misto* or boiled meat, consists of beef, ham, chicken, sausage and tongue served with a pungent green sauce.

If you have a chance in the hill-towns of the Marches, order *porchetta*, a succulent, spit-roasted suckling pig. You'll also see all shapes and sizes of sausage offered as main dishes.

The Adriatic region abounds in delicious vegetables. Depending on the season, you'll be offered asparagus—both green and white—artichokes, mushrooms of many varieties, plum tomatoes, green peas and beans, spinach, red chicory from Treviso, and several types of unfamiliar lettuce that make good salads. *Porcini*, giant boletus mushrooms, are a great delicacy served grilled or marinated in oil. To go with your meat dish, try *zucchini ripieni*, stuffed courgettes or *insalata di mozzarella*, a tomato salad with slices of mozzarella cheese.

Cheese, Fruit and Desserts

You will, of course, find the familiar Italian **cheeses** along the Adriatic—like *ricotta*—but be sure to try as well some of the varieties that aren't available back home. Italians use parmesan to sprinkle over pasta, but they also eat the best of it *(parmigiano* or *parmigiano reggiano)* as is. The texture is grainy, the flavour subtle and tangy. *Asiago* from Friuli, belongs to the parmesan family, as does the greenish-yellow *venezza* from Venice. *Liptauer* cheese is a speciality of Trieste. Bland mozzarella served uncooked with tomatoes, basil and olive oil is delicious.

Fruit is a great favourite after a copious meal in Italy, and when you see the choice and quality of succulent fruit you'll probably follow suit. Peaches, apricots, figs, melon, cherries and grapes are available in summer. A slice of watermelon bought on the street makes a nice mid-afternoon refresher.

As elsewhere in the country, you'll find a profusion of **cakes** and **tarts** to round off the meal. Among the more interesting is the *zuppa inglese*—

Tangy cheese, cool wine: good on their own, better still together.

not a soup at all but a trifle. *Granita* is a partially frozen dessert made with coffee or fruit juice. In the Friuli region be sure to sample the strudel, apple or apricot or almond. Finally, as every schoolboy knows, Italian **ice cream** is hard to resist.

Coffee, Wine and Water

Italians invariably end their meal with an espresso **coffee,** very strong and black, served in a demi-tasse cup. If you want coffee with milk, order a *cappuccino* or, at breakfast, a large cup of *caffè latte. Caffè lungo,* less concentrated, is made with more water. *Caffè corretto* contains a shot of *grappa* or other alcohol.

Italian **wines** need no introduction. Some very good ones come from the vineyards of the northern Adriatic—and they tend to be less expensive than the wines of Piedmont and Tuscany.

The Veneto region produces the ruby Valpolicella and the light-red Bardolino, as well as Cabernet, Merlot and the excellent white Soave. Around Padua you're likely to find some pleasant red and white wines from the Euganean Hills. Friuli has several fine whites—Pinot Bianco and Pinot Grigio and the tasty Tocai

(not to be confused with the sweet Hungarian wine of the same name).

In Romagna, try the dark-red Sangiovese, the white Albana and Trebbiano. The sparkling red Lambrusco, often served chilled, goes very well with the rich food of the region. The Marches is famous for its white Verdicchio, a wine with a rather high alcohol content (up to 14%) that comes in an unusual vase-shaped bottle.

With meals, Italians tend to order bottled mineral **water** *acqua minerale,* either with bubbles *(gasata)* or without *(naturale).* But local tap water is perfectly drinkable, just ask for *acqua normale.*

Before and After

Before a meal, Italians often take a Campari, or a vermouth like Punt e Mes or a Cinzano. After-dinner drinks include Amaro or Amaretto, made from almonds; Sambuca, an anise-flavoured sweet liqueur; the potent *grappa,* an eau-de-vie distilled from the residue of grapes; and in the Trieste area, *slivowitz,* a plum brandy, similar to its neighbouring Yugoslav cousin. The tiny republic of San Marino has a reputable dessert wine, Moscato, and Udine produces the sweet Piccolit.

To Help You Order...

What do you recommend?
Do you have a set menu?

Cosa consiglia?
Avete un menù a prezzo fisso?

I'd like a/an/some...

Vorrei...

beer	**una birra**	napkin	**un tovagliolo**
bread	**del pane**	pepper	**del pepe**
butter	**del burro**	potatoes	**delle patate**
coffee	**un caffè**	salad	**dell'insalata**
cream	**della panna**	salt	**del sale**
fish	**del pesce**	soup	**una minestra**
fruit	**della frutta**	sugar	**dello zucchero**
ice cream	**un gelato**	tea	**un tè**
meat	**della carne**	(iced) water	**dell'acqua (fredda)**
milk	**del latte**	wine	**del vino**

...and Read the Menu

aglio	garlic	**manzo**	beef
agnello	lamb	**mela**	apple
albicocche	apricots	**melanzana**	aubergine
aragosta	spiny lobster	**merluzzo**	cod
arancia	orange	**ostrica**	oyster
bistecca	beef steak	**pancetta**	bacon
braciola	chop	**peperoni**	peppers, pimentos
brodetto	fish soup		
bue	beef	**pesca**	peach
calamari	squid	**pesce**	fish
carciofi	artichokes	**piselli**	peas
cavolo	cabbage	**pollo**	chicken
cicoria	endive	**pomodoro**	tomato
cipolle	onions	**prosciutto**	ham
coniglio	rabbit	**rognoni**	kidneys
cozze	mussels	**salsa**	sauce
crostacei	shellfish	**sarde**	sardines
fagioli	beans	**sogliola**	sole
fegato	liver	**stufato**	stew
fichi	figs	**tonno**	tunny (tuna)
formaggio	cheese	**uova**	eggs
funghi	mushrooms	**uva**	grapes
gamberi	scampi, prawns	**vitello**	veal
lamponi	raspberries	**vongole**	clams

99

BLUEPRINT for a Perfect Trip

How to Get There

Because of the complexity and variability of the many fares, you should ask the advice of an informed travel agent well before your departure.

BY AIR

Scheduled flights

Venice's Marco Polo airport is on several European routes. Travellers from further afield will normally have to fly to a European capital for connecting flights to Venice. Rome and Milan are the main gateways to Italy, both for international and intercontinental flights, and from these airports there are daily connections to Venice, Trieste and Rimini (Milan–Venice takes about 45 minutes). Flight time from London to Venice is about 2 hours, from New York to Milan approximately 7½ hours.

Charter flights and package tours

From North America: Almost all 15-day tours to Italy feature stopovers in Milan or Venice. Tours of 11 days often include Venice, as well as Rome and Florence. In addition to the transatlantic air fare, these tours provide de luxe or first class hotel accomodation, airport and hotel transfers, baggage handling, meals as specified in each itinerary, some or all sightseeing, the services of a guide and taxis.

From the U.K. and Ireland: Tour operators offer a variety of one- or two-week inclusive holidays, either visiting a particular town or taking in a series of places. You have choice of hotel or selfcatering accommodation. Packages must be booked in advance. It's wise to purchase insurance; most firms are reliable, but there is always the possibility that something may go wrong.

At present, the only charter flights from London operate to Rimini. **101**

BY CAR

The principal car-ferry routes are: 1) via France: Dover–Boulogne/Calais/Dunkirk; Folkstone–Boulogne/Calais; Newhaven–Dieppe; Southampton–Cherbourg/Le Havre; Ramsgate–Dunkirk; 2) via Belgium: Dover–Ostend/Zeebrugge; Folkestone–Ostend; Felixstowe/Hull–Zeebrugge; 3) via Holland: Harwich–Hook van Holland; Hull–Rotterdam; Sheerness–Vlissingen. For a slightly higher price than the ferry, you can cross by hovercraft from Dover to Calais or Boulogne. Make sure of your passage by booking the ferry ticket well in advance.

You can follow toll motorways (expressways) through most of France to the Italian border, then continue eastward to the Adriatic on the *autostrada*. It's also possible for you and your car to travel by motorail from Boulogne or Paris to Milan. British Rail will have the details.

BY TRAIN

A through-train from London to Rimini operates only in summer. At other times of the year, you must change at Milan and Bologna. Change at Bologna to reach Ravenna or Ferrara.

Eurailpasses, Inter-Rail Cards and Rail Europ Senior Cards are all valid in Italy. In addition, the Italian State Railways offer special discount tickets for travel within the country. Enquire at any travel agency.

When to Go

The beach areas of the northern Adriatic coast have only one season that stretches from the end of May or early June to mid- or end-September, when the temperature permits swimming. Before or after this period, most hotels are closed, with the seaside resorts and beaches practically deserted. As for cities like Venice and Bologna, they work their magic on visitors all year round. The best time to visit, however, is in spring or autumn—between April and June and again in September—when the weather is most pleasant and the streets less crowded. Average monthly minimum temperatures (Venice area):

Air temperature	J	F	M	A	M	J	J	A	S	O	N	D
°F	34	34	41	51	57	64	68	66	62	52	43	37
°C	1	1	5	10	14	18	20	19	17	11	6	3

Planning Your Budget

To give you an idea of what to expect, here are some average prices in Italian lire (L.). However, remember that all prices must be regarded as *approximate* and that the inflation rate is high.

Airport transfer. Public bus from Venice Airport to Piazzale Roma L. 500, airline bus L. 3,500.

Baby-sitters. L. 14,000–20,000 per hour.

Camping (high season). Adults L. 6,000 per person per night, children L. 5,000, caravan (trailer) or camper L. 10,000, tent and car L. 6,500, motorbike L. 2,500.

Car hire (international company). *Fiat Panda 45* L. 38,500 per day, L. 600 per km., L. 592,000 per week with unlimited mileage. *Alfa 33* L. 67,800 per day, L. 820 per km., L. 940,000 per week with unlimited mileage. Add. 18% tax.

Cigarettes (packet of 20). Italian brands L. 1,600 and up, imported brands L. 2,500–3,000.

Entertainment. Cinema L. 5,000–7,000, discotheque (entry and one drink) L. 15,000–30,000.

Hairdressers. *Woman's* shampoo and set or blow-dry L. 18,000–27,000, permanent wave L. 45,000–70,000. *Man's* haircut L. 12,000–15,000, L. 20,000 with shampoo.

Hotels (double room with bath, summer season, including tax and services). ***** L. 400,000–600,000, **** L. 130,000–380,000, *** L. 70,000–240,000, ** L. 45,000–190,000, * L. 30,000–100,000.

Meals and drinks. Continental breakfast L. 7,000–15,000, lunch/dinner in fairly good establishment L. 35,000–80,000, coffee served at a table L. 2,500–4,500, served at the bar L. 600–800, bottle of wine L. 4,500 and up, soft drink L. 1,500 and up, aperitif L. 2,500 and up.

Museums. L. 1,000–7,000.

Shopping bag. 500 g. of bread L. 1,000–1,900, 250 g. butter L. 2,000 and up, 6 eggs L. 1,200 and up, 500 g. of beefsteak L. 8,000 and up, 250 g. coffee L. 3,000 and up, bottle of wine L. 3,000 and up.

Youth hostels. Approx. L. 10,000 per night with breakfast, L. 6,500 per meal.

An A–Z Summary of Practical Information and Facts

A star (*) following an entry indicates that relevant prices are to be found on p. 103.

Listed after many entries is the appropriate Italian translation, usually in the singular, plus a number of phrases that should help you when seeking assistance.

A **ACCOMMODATION*.** The range of accommodation in the Adriatic coast area varies from de luxe hotels *(albergo* or *hotel)* to modest inns *(locanda)* and boarding houses *(pensione)*. Rimini alone—Europe's biggest seaside resort—has more than 1,600 hotels. Other types of accommodation on the coast include villas *(villa)*, flats *(appartamento)*, bungalows *(bungalow* or *residence)*, spa resorts *(località termale)*, campsites (see separate entry) and children's holiday homes *(colonia)*.

You should book in advance for the tourist season (for Venice, it is a must)—particularly for the month of August—although you'll usually find something, even at the last minute, with the assistance of the local tourist office. Hotel prices in the Rimini area run about 20% lower than those of other Italian resorts—while Venice rates are about 10% higher than the average. Some hotels insist on guests taking at least one full meal per day on the premises; other hotels offer half-board or just bed and breakfast. If you ask for board-and-lodging rates, your stay may have to be a minimum three days. Most hotels along the Adriatic are closed in winter. Those that are not usually have an off-season rate, so be sure to check.

Service charge, tourist tax and VAT, or sales tax, are often included in the room rate. When leaving your hotel, remember to take the receipt of the payment with you as in restaurants (see p. 94).

Youth hostels *(ostello della gioventù)*. There are several youth hostels in the Adriatic coast region: at Ferrara, Lido di Iesolo, Pesaro, Rimini-Miramare, Trieste-Grignano, Venice-Giudecca and further inland at Bologna. They are open to holders of membership cards issued by the International Youth Hostels Federation, or by the A.I.G. *(Associazione Italiana Alberghi per la Gioventù)*, the Italian Youth Hostels Association, at:

Quadrato della Concordia, 9, 00144 Rome

AIRPORTS *(aeroporto)*. The northern Adriatic coast is served by three major airports; Venice-Marco Polo, Rimini-Miramare and Trieste-Ronchi dei Legionari. (Bologna Airport, Borgo Panigale, is also within easy reach.)

Venice and Rimini airports handle domestic and international flights, and are equipped with restaurants and snack bars, souvenir shops, news-stands, currency exchange offices *(cambio)* and duty-free shops. Porters are usually available, or if you're lucky, you'll find a luggage trolley at Marco Polo Airport. Trieste's tiny airport handles domestic and charter flights.

Ground transport*. From Marco Polo, buses run the 13 kilometres to Piazzale Roma car park in Venice about once an hour. There's also a motorboat service (a 30-minute trip) between the airport and Piazza San Marco, which coincides with flight departures and arrivals.

At Rimini, public buses connect Miramare Airport with the main railway station on Piazzale C. Battisti, 7 kilometres to the north, and airport buses run to the town terminal at Piazzale Tripoli.

In the north-east at Trieste, public buses run frequently between Ronchi dei Legionari and the Stazione Centrale in the centre of town, a distance of 35 kilometres.

BICYCLE HIRE *(noleggio biciclette)*. Bicycles are increasingly popular in the Adriatic resort areas. Ask your hotel receptionist or any tourist office for the address of a rental firm.

CAMPING* *(campeggio)*. Campsites are listed in the yellow pages of the telephone directory either under "Campeggio" or "Campeggi-Ostelli–Villaggi Turistici". You can also contact the tourist office (see TOURIST INFORMATION OFFICES) for a comprehensive list of sites, rates and complete details. The Touring Club Italiano and the Automobile Club d'Italia publish lists of campsites and tourist villages, which can be bought in bookstores of referred to in tourist offices.

In Italy, you may camp freely outside of sites if you obtain permission either from the owner of the property or from the local authorities but it's wisest to chose a place where there are other campers.

If you enter Italy with a caravan (trailer) you must be able to show an inventory (with two copies) of the material and equipment in the caravan: dishes, linen, etc.

May we camp here? **Possiamo campeggiare qui?**
Is there a campsite near here? **C'è un campeggio qui vicino?**

A

B

C

C **CAR HIRE*** *(autonoleggio).* Major car rental firms and scores of small private operators vie for the tourist trade. They're all listed in the yellow pages of the telephone book, and many hotels have arrangements with an agency. A valid driving licence is needed to hire a car, insurance is mandatory and a deposit is usually required (except for holders of major credit cards). Minimum age varies from 18 to 25 according to the company. Large agencies will let you leave a rented car in another Italian or European city for an additional fee.

I'd like to rent a car (tomorrow).	**Vorrei noleggiare un'automobile (per domani).**
for one day	**per un giorno**
a week	**una settimana**

CIGARETTES, CIGARS, TOBACCO* *(sigarette, sigari, tabacco).* Sold under state monopoly, tobacco products in Italy are price-controlled. Dark and light tobaccos are available, as are most well-known cigars and pipe tobacco. The cheapest Italian cigarettes are considered somewhat rough by most foreigners. Local and imported brands are on sale in tobacco shops *(tabaccaio)* bearing a large white "T" on a dark-blue background, not at kiosks, although hotel news-stands may have some cigarettes. "T" shops also sell postcards and stamps.

Vietato fumare means "no smoking", and you'll find the sign in buses, some taxis and many public places.

I'd like a packet of ...	**Vorrei un pacchetto di ...**
with/without filter	**con/senza filtro**
mild/strong cigarettes	**delle sigarette leggere/forti**
I'd like a box of matches.	**Per favore, mi dia una scatola di fiammiferi.**

CLOTHING. From May to September, wear light-weight cotton clothes and take along a light wrap or jacket for the evening. Comfortable walking shoes are indispensable when visiting cities. In spring, autumn and winter, heavier clothing is necessary.

Adriatic Italians are accustomed to the informality of foreign visitors, and few restaurants insist on a jacket and tie. In casinos, however, ties may be required. Slacks for women are suitable everywhere, but shorts or barebacked dresses are forbidden in churches.

Most Adriatic resorts consider themselves family gathering places, and thus nudity is normally not permitted.

COMMUNICATIONS

Post offices *(posta* or *ufficio postale)* handle telegrams, mail and money transfers, and some have public telephones. Postage stamps are also sold at tobacconists *(tabaccaio)* and at some hotel desks. Post boxes are red.

Post office **hours** are normally from 8.30 a.m. to 2 p.m., Monday to Friday, until noon or 1 p.m. on Saturdays.

Poste restante (general delivery). Unless it's absolutely essential, don't arrange to receive mail during a brief visit to Italy: have people cable or telephone your hotel, it's more reliable. You can nevertheless have your mail addressed c/o *Fermo Posta* (poste restante or general delivery) to the main post office *(posta centrale)* of the town in which you are going to stay. A small charge is made. Take your passport along as identification when you go to pick up mail from the post office.

Telegrams. Night letters, or night-rate telegrams *(lettera telegramma),* which arrive the next morning, are far cheaper than ordinary cables but can only be sent overseas.

Telephone *(telefono).* To make an international call, go to the main post office in the larger towns where there are operator services. Your hotel will also get the number for you, of course, but it will cost a little more. Either way, the long-distance lines are often overloaded, so be prepared for a long wait.

Public phones take either coins or tokens *(gettone),* which you obtain at a bar (the barman will buy back any you don't use). Armed with a good quantity of coins or *gettoni,* you can dial direct from any phone booth either abroad or within Italy. See the telephone directory for code numbers. First, insert a coin, lift the receiver, and wait. There may be silence for quite a while before you get the dial tone, a series of regular dash-dash-dash sounds. (A dot-dot-dot sequence means the exchange is overloaded, in which case you must hang up and try again.) If the dot-dot-dot sound breaks in when you are dialling a number, it means that one of the telephone lines along the way is busy so you have to start all over again.

A few usefull numbers:

Domestic directory inquiries	12
Operator for Europe	15
Operator for intercontinental calls	170
Telegrams	186
Telephone assistance service (see TOURIST INFORMATION OFFICES)	116

C

Give me … *gettoni*, please.	**Per favore, mi dia … gettoni.**
Can you get me this number in …?	**Può passarmi questo numero a …?**
Have you received any mail for …?	**C'è posta per …?**
I'd like a stamp for this letter/postcard.	**Desidero un francobollo per questa lettera/cartolina.**
express (special delivery)	**espresso**
airmail	**via aerea**
registered	**raccomandata**
I want to send a telegram to …	**Desidero mandare un telegramma a …**

COMPLAINTS. In hotels, restaurants or shops, complaints should be made to the manager or proprietor. If satisfaction is not quickly forthcoming, mention your intention to report the incident to the local tourist association or to the police for more serious matters. The threat of a formal declaration to the police should be effective in such cases as overcharging for car repairs. Threatening to call your embassy or consulate will impress few, although this should be your first course of action if you get into any real trouble with the police, as in a major car accident. Arguments over taxi fares can usually be settled by checking the notices in taxis specifying supplementary charges (airport runs, holiday rates, night surcharges, etc.). Generally speaking, try to come to an agreement in advance.

CONSULATES and EMBASSIES (*consolato; ambasciata*)

Australia	Via Alessandria, 215, Rome; tel. 84 12 41
Canada	Via G. Battista De Rossi, 27, Rome; tel. 85 53 41/4
Eire	Largo del Nazareno, 3, Rome; tel. 678 25 41
South Africa	Piazza Monte Grappa, 4, Rome; tel. 360 84 41
United Kingdom	Dorsoduro, 1051, Venice; tel. 2 72 07
	Via XX Settembre, 80, Rome; tel. 475 54 41
U.S.A.	Via Roma, 9, P.O.B. 604, Trieste; tel. 6 87 28
	Via Vittorio Veneto, 119, Rome; tel. 46 741

COURTESIES. Italians observe certain formal courtesies. For instance, when entering a shop or office, or even a taxi, the usual greeting is *buon giorno* (good morning) or *buona sera* (good evening). When asking someone a question, it is customary to preface it with *per favore* or *per piacere* (please), and always remember to say *grazie* (thanks) or *grazie mille* (thank you very much), to which one responds *prego* (you're welcome, don't mention it).

Introductions are usually accompanied by handshaking and the phrase *piacere* (it's a pleasure). With people you know, *ciao* is the casual form of greeting or farewell; *arrivederci* is the more appropriate expression for "good-bye".

Mi scusi is what you say when you want something repeated, *permesso* when you want to excuse yourself in getting past someone.

A woman should totally ignore any form of greeting from an unknown man—unless, that is, she is interested in him. And to make a hit with an Italian parent, compliment them on their children, the surest form of flattery in the country.

| How are you? | **Come sta?** |
| Fine, thank you. | **Bene, grazie.** |

CRIME and THEFT. Violent crime against foreigners is infrequent along the Adriatic. Women are rarely physically molested, unless an Italian man has misunderstood unintentional provocation (but accepting a ride in a total stranger's car, for example, might come under that heading).

But petty crime is increasing everywhere in Italy, and tourists are always easy targets for robbery. By taking a few simple precautions, you can reduce the risk:

- leave your documents and unneeded cash at your hotel, preferably in the safe

- carry as much of your money as possible in the form of traveller's cheques, and keep a record of these (and your passport) separate from the cheques themselves

- don't leave your handbag slung loosely over your street-side shoulder; it can be ripped off by thieves on motorbikes or in cars

- never leave valuables (bags, etc.) unattended or behind your back (at airports, railway stations, restaurants, on beaches, etc.) even for a few seconds

- never leave anything of value in your car, not even in the boot (trunk), particularly in urban areas. Keep any car containing luggage in a safe place, preferably looked after by a parking attendant, when you're not actually at the wheel.

C And if you *are*, in fact, robbed, report it to the police *(carabinieri)* immediately—for insurance purposes if nothing else: your insurance company will need to see a copy of the police report (as will your consulate if your passport is stolen). As for stolen or lost traveller's cheques, report the matter at once to the bank that issued them so that payment can be stopped immediately.

CUSTOMS *(dogana)* **and ENTRY REGULATIONS.** For a stay of up to three months, a valid passport is sufficient for citizens of Australia, Canada, New Zealand and U.S.A. Visitors from Eire and the United Kingdom need only an identity card to enter Italy. Tourists from South Africa must have a visa.

Here's what you can take into Italy duty-free and, when returning home, into your own country:

Entering Italy from:	Cigarettes		Cigars		Tobacco	Spirits		Wine
1)	200	or	50	or	250 g.	¾ l.	or	2 l.
2)	300	or	75	or	400 g.	1.5 l	and	4 l.
3)	400	or	100	or	500 g.	¾ l.	or	2 l.
Into:								
Australia	200	or	250 g.	or	250 g.	1 l.	or	1 l.
Canada	200	and	50	and	900 g.	1.1 l.	or	1.1 l.
Eire	200	or	50		250 g.	1.1 l.	and	2 l.
N. Zealand	200	or	50	or	250 g.	1.5 l.	and	4.5 l.
S. Africa	400	and	50	and	250 g.	1 l.	or	2 l.
U.K.	200	or	50	or	250 g.	1 l.	and	2 l.
U.S.A.	200	and	100	and	4)	1 l.	or	1 l.

1) within Europe from non-EEC countries
2) within Europe from EEC countries
3) countries outside Europe
4) a reasonable quantity

Currency restrictions. Non-residents may import or export up to L. 500,000 in local currency. In foreign currencies, you may import unlimited amounts, but to take the equivalent of more than L. 5,000,000 in or out of the country, you must fill out a V2 declaration form at the border upon entry.

I've nothing to declare.	**Non ho nulla da dichiarare.**
It's for personal use.	**È per mio uso personale.**

DRIVING IN ITALY. To bring your car into Italy, you will need:

- an International Driving Licence or a valid national licence
- car registration papers
- Green Card (an extension to your regular insurance policy, making it valid specifically for Italy)
- a red warning triangle in case of breakdown
- national identity sticker for your car

Note: Before leaving home, check with your automobile association about the latest regulations concerning *petrol coupons* (that give tourists access to cheaper fuel) in Italy, as they are constantly changing.

Driving conditions. Traffic on major roads has right of way over traffic entering from side-roads, but this, like other traffic regulations, is frequently ignored, so beware. At intersections of roads of similar importance, the car on the right theoretically has the right of way. When passing other vehicles, or remaining in the left-hand (passing) lane, keep your directional indicator flashing. Italian drivers are impulsive and have quick reflexes. They expect others to drive like they do, so keep alert in traffic, particularly in the cities, and be prepared for anything.

The motorways, or expressways *(autostrada),* are designed for fast and safe driving; each section requires the payment of a toll: you collect a card from an automatic machine or from the booth attendant and pay at the other end for the distance travelled. Try to stock up on coins and small banknotes, since the toll booth attendants don't like making change.

On country roads and even many main highways, you'll encounter bicycles, motorscooters, three-wheeled vehicles, horse-drawn carts and even donkey caravans. Very often, such slow-moving vehicles have *no* lights, an obvious danger from dusk to dawn.

D   Last but not least: cars, buses, lorries (trucks) make use, indiscrimi-
nately, of their horns. In fact, blowing one's horn is an Italian attitude,
so don't get flustered if it's done at you, and blow your own horn
whenever it could help to warn of your impending arrival.

Speed limits. Speed limits in Italy are based on the car engine size.
The following chart gives the engine size in cubic centimetres, and the
limits (in kilometres per hour):

Engine size	less than 600 cc.	600 to 900 cc.	900 to 1300 cc. (and motorcycles more than 150 cc.)	more than 1300 cc.
Main roads	80 kph.	90 kph.	100 kph.	110 kph.
Motorways	90 kph.	110 kph.	130 kph.	140 kph.

Town speed limits are posted on the entry roads in kilometres per
hour.

Traffic police *(polizia stradale).* When seen—not very often—Italian
traffic police use motorcycles or Alfa Romeos, usually light blue. All
cities and many towns and villages have signs posted at the outskirts
indicating at least the telephone number of the local traffic police or
the *carabinieri.* Speeding fines can often be paid on the spot, but ask
for a receipt *(ricevuta).*

Breakdowns. Garages are everywhere, and major towns have agencies
specializing in foreign cars. You can dial 116 for emergency service
from the Automobile Club d'Italia. Call boxes are located at regular
intervals on the *autostrade.*

Fuel and oil. Fuel, sold at government-set price levels, comes as super
(98–100 octane), lead-free (still rare, 95 octane) and normal (86–88
octane). Diesel is also usually available. Oil comes in at least three
varieties.

Parking. There's generally no problem finding parking places along
the Adriatic—except near crowded beach resorts. For safety's sake
you are advised to park in a lot with an attendant or in a hotel's
secured zone. In Venice, the Piazzale Roma is the closest you can get
to the centre by car. It has two large, multi-level garages. However, a
112 huge car park exists on the adjacent island of Tronchetto, connected

from May to October by public water-bus service to the centre of the city. It's also possible to park at the Lido, Mestre, San Giuliano and Fusina.

Road signs. Most road signs employed in Italy are international pictographs, but here are some written ones you might come across:

Accendere le luci	Use headlights
Caduta massi	Falling rocks
Curva pericolosa	Dangerous bend (curve)
Deviazione	Diversion (Detour)
Discesa pericolosa	Steep hill
Divieto di sorpasso	No overtaking (passing)
Divieto di sosta	No stopping
Lavori in corso	Road works (Men working)
Parcheggio autorizzato	Parking allowed
Passaggio a livello	Level crossing
Pericolo	Danger
Rallentare	Slow down
Senso vietato/unico	No entry/One-way street

(International) Driving Licence	**patente (internazionale)**
Car registration papers	**libretto di circolazione**
Green Card	**carta verde**
Full tank please, ...	**Per favore, faccia il pieno di ...**
super/normal	**super/normale**
unleaded/diesel	**senza piombo/gasolio**
Check the oil/tires/battery.	**Controlli l'olio/i pneumatici/ la batteria.**
I've had a breakdown.	**Ho avuto un guasto.**
There's been an accident.	**C'è stato un incidente.**

DRUGS. For those convicted of possessing or selling drugs in Italy, the possibility of severe penalties and considerable time in prison await them. Italian law does not differentiate between hard and soft drugs. Maximum sentences are about eight years in prison and/or very heavy fines. Italian police keep an eye on hangouts of young people where drugs might be circulating. And once arrested on a drug charge, a person may spend as long as a year in jail before being even formally charged because of the jammed backlog of court cases. Foreign embassies and consulates say they are unable to do much for citizens arrested on drug charges. The wise tourist will be forewarned. **113**

E **ELECTRICITY.** Electricity of two voltages—110–130 and 220—is supplied in Italy, with different plugs and sockets for each. The voltage is generally indicated on the sockets in hotels, but it's best to ask to avoid ruining your shaver or hairdryer.

What's the voltage, 220 or 110?	**Qual è il voltaggio, 220 (duecentoventi) o 110 (centodieci)?**
I'd like an adaptor/a battery.	**Vorrei una presa complementare/ una batteria.**

EMERGENCIES. Emergency telephone numbers differ from city to city, but are listed at the front pages of directories. Some numbers, however, are nationwide:

Police, all-purpose emergency number	113
Road assistance (Automobile Club d'Italia) and telephone assistance service (see TOURIST INFORMATION OFFICES)	116

Depending on the nature of the problem, see also separate entries such as CONSULATES AND EMBASSIES, MEDICAL CARE, POLICE, etc.

Careful	**Attenzione**	Police	**Polizia**
Fire	**Incendio**	Stop	**Stop**
Help	**Aiuto**	Stop thief	**Al ladro**

Please, can you place an emergency call for me to the …?	**Per favore, può fare per me una telefonata d'emergenza …?**
police/fire brigade/hospital	**alla polizia/ai pompieri/ all'ospedale**

G **GUIDES and TOURS.** Your hotel should be able to arrange for an experienced guide to accompany you. At most major tourist attractions you'll find coin-operated machines, some equipped with coloured slides, which provide taped descriptions of what you're seeing—in four or five languages.

The Italian tourist agency, CIT *(Compagnia Italiana Turismo)*, and private firms offer guided tours on foot and by boat within Venice and the lagoon.

Day-long excursions from major resort areas include trips to Venice, Bologna, Verona and Florence. Your travel agent or hotel receptionist can recommend chauffeurs with private cars if you so wish.

We'd like an English-speaking guide.	**Desideriamo una guida che parla inglese.**
I need an English interpreter.	**Ho bisogno di un interprete d'inglese.**

HAIRDRESSERS and BARBERS* *(parrucchiere; barbiere)*. Italian
hairdressers deserve their reputation for excellence. Men can usually
find an empty chair without much of a wait. But it is better for women
to make an appointment. It's customary to tip a barber 10–15%. La-
dies should not tip the owner of a salon, but the shampooer, manicur-
ist or stylist should receive up to 15% of the bill.

I'd like a shampoo and set.	**Vorrei shampo e messa in piega.**
haircut	**il taglio**
blow-dry	**asciugatura al fon**
colour rinse	**un riflesso**
manicure	**la manicure**
Don't cut it too short.	**Non li tagli troppo corti.**
A little more off (here).	**Un po' di più (qui).**

HITCH-HIKING *(autostop)*. Many people hitch-hike in Italy, especially in the summer—even on the motorways despite signs forbid-
ding the practice at the entrances to *autostrade*. Lots of young people
travel around the Adriatic coast this way, but a girl travelling alone is
advised not to hitch-hike.

Can you give me/give us a lift to …?	**Può darmi/darci un passaggio fino a …?**

LANGUAGE. Almost all hotels along the coast have personnel who
speak at least a smattering of English, French or German. Similarly,
most shopkeepers can understand enough in other languages to con-
duct transactions.

In Italian it's important to remember that the letter "c" is often pronounced like "ch"—when it is followed by an "e" or "i"—while the
letters "ch" together sound like the "c" in cat. Thus *cento* (hundred)
comes out as CHEHN-toa but *conto* (bill) is pronounced KOAN-toa and
chiesa (church), KYAI-zah.

The Berlitz phrase book ITALIAN FOR TRAVELLERS covers most situations you are likely to encounter in Italy; also useful is the Italian-
English/English-Italian pocket dictionary, containing a special menu-
reader supplement.

Do you speak English?	**Parla inglese?**
I don't speak Italian.	**Non parlo italiano.**

115

L **LAUNDRY and DRY-CLEANING** *(lavanderia; tintoria).* Along the Adriatic you'll find plenty of launderettes where you do it yourself or for a slight extra charge leave it with an attendant. Some launderettes also iron or handle dry-cleaning. Otherwise take dry-cleaning to a *tintoria,* which will have normal and express service. Hotels, too, handle laundry, often with same-day service, but the rates are higher.

LOST PROPERTY *(oggetti smarriti).* Check with the Ufficio Oggetti Smarriti at the local police station and the tourist office, or try to trace lost property through the railway, taxi company, or other.

It's a good idea to take out property insurance in your own country for the duration of your holiday in Italy. If you lose something on your trip, report the loss to the local police and obtain a document to show to your insurance company on your return (see also CRIME AND THEFT).

I've lost my passport/wallet/ handbag.	**Ho perso il passaporto/ portafoglio/la borsetta.**

M **MAPS.** A broad range of maps of the area can be found at newsstands and bookshops. They come in a wide range of prices. The tourist offices also produce colourful maps—many of them free of charge. For road maps, look in the corner for the date to see that you get an up-to-date one.

The maps in this book were prepared by Falk-Verlag, Hamburg, that also publish a map of Italy.

I'd like a street plan of …	**Vorrei una piantina di …**
a road map of this region	**una carta stradale di questa regione**

MEDICAL CARE. If your health insurance does not honour bills from foreign countries, you can take out a special short-term policy for your trip. Visitors from Great Britain have the right to claim public health services available to Italians since both countries are members of the E.E.C. Before leaving home get a copy of the requisite form from the Department of Health and Social Security.

If you're in need of medical care, it's best to ask your hotel receptionist to help you find a doctor (or dentist) who speaks English.

The first-aid *(pronto soccorso)* section of municipal hospitals can **116** handle medical emergencies satisfactorily. Call 113 for an ambulance.

Pharmacies. The Italian *farmacia* is open during shopping hours. The opening schedule for duty pharmacies is posted on every pharmacy door and recorded in the local papers.

|---|---|
I need a doctor/ a dentist.	**Ho bisogno di un medico/ dentista.**
I've a pain here.	**Ho un dolore qui.**
a stomach ache	**il mal di stomaco**
a fever	**la febbre**
a sunburn	**una scottatura di sole**

MONEY MATTERS

Currency. The *lira* (plural: *lire,* abbreviated *L.* or *Lit.*) is Italy's monetary unit.

Coins: L. 5, 10, 20, 50, 100, 200 and 500.
Banknotes: L. 1,000, 2,000, 5,000, 10,000, 50,000 and 100,000.
For currency restrictions, see CUSTOMS AND ENTRY REGULATIONS.

Banks *(banca)* are open from 8.30 a.m. to 1.30 p.m. (11.30 a.m. on local "semi-holidays"), Monday to Friday. They close on public holidays and weekends.

Currency exchange offices *(cambio)* reopen after the siesta, usually until at least 6.30 p.m.; some are open on Saturday.

Exchange rates for hard currency are never as good at a *cambio* as at the bank—but you'll do much better than at your hotel. Passports are sometimes required when exchanging money.

Credit cards and traveller's cheques. Major hotels, many shops and some restaurants take credit cards. Traveller's cheques are accepted almost everywhere, but it's much better to exchange your cheques for lire at a bank or *cambio*.

Eurocheques are easily cashed in Italy.

Prices. Italy has a high rate of inflation, and prices along the Adriatic reflect this, particularly in cities like Venice. However, public transport and entry fees to museums are quite reasonable, and there are still bargains to be had if you shop around. It is wise to order local dishes, wines, beers and spirits; you'll pay a lot for imported drinks. In bars or cafés, sitting down and having a waiter bring your espresso may cost five times as much as having it at the counter.

M I want to change some pounds/ dollars. — **Desidero cambiare delle sterline/ dei dollari.**

Do you accept traveller's cheques? — **Accetta traveller's cheques?**

Can I pay with this credit card? — **Posso pagare con la carta di credito?**

How much is this? — **Quanto costa questo?**

N **NEWSPAPERS and MAGAZINES** *(giornale; rivista).* Most resorts or towns have at least one news-stand which sells foreign language newspapers and magazines, though prices are high and deliveries are always at least one day behind publication date. Most also sell news-magazines.

Have you any English-language newspapers? — **Avete giornali in inglese?**

P **PHOTOGRAPHY.** Major brands of film are available in photographic shops throughout the country, though they are often more expensive than elsewhere. You may prefer to take film back home with you for processing, as it usually takes some time on the spot. Never leave a camera in a car, or unattended anywhere.

The use of ordinary flash is permitted in most public buildings, but ask at the entrance.

Some airport security machines use X-rays which can ruin your film. Ask that it be checked separately, or enclose it in a lead-lined bag.

I'd like a film for this camera. — **Vorrei una pellicola per questa macchina fotografica.**

a black-and-white film — **una pellicola in bianco e nero**
a colour-slide film — **una pellicola per diapositive**
a film for colour prints — **una pellicola per fotografie a colori**

How long will it take to develop this film? — **Quanto tempo ci vuole per sviluppare questa pellicola?**

May I take a picture? — **Posso fare una fotografia?**

POLICE. The city police, *Vigili Urbani,* handle traffic, hand out parking fines and perform other routine police tasks.

The *Carabinieri*, a paramilitary force, wear light-brown or blue uniforms and peaked caps, and deal with violent or serious crimes and demonstrations.

Outside of towns, the *Polizia Stradale* patrol the highways and byways (see under DRIVING).

The universal police emergency number is 113.

Where's the nearest police station?	**Dov'è il più vicino posto di polizia?**

PUBLIC HOLIDAYS *(festa)*. On all national holidays, banks, government institutions, most shops and some museums are closed. Along the northern part of the Adriatic coast, the August *Ferragosto* holiday does not—as in other parts of Italy—occasion a week-long shutdown.

January 1	*Capodanno* or *Primo dell'Anno*	New Year's Day
January 6	*Epifania*	Epiphany
April 25	*Festa della Liberazione*	Liberation Day
May 1	*Festa del Lavoro*	Labour Day
August 15	*Ferragosto*	Assumption Day
November 1	*Ognissanti*	All Saints' Day
December 8	*L'Immacolata Concezione*	Immaculate Conception
December 25	*Natale*	Christmas Day
December 26	*Santo Stefano*	St. Stephen's Day
Movable date:	*Lunedì di Pasqua*	Easter Monday

Are you open tomorrow?	**È aperto domani?**

RADIO and TV *(radio; televisione)*. During the tourist season, RAI, the Italian state radio and TV network, occasionally broadcasts news in English, predominantly about Italian affairs. Vatican Radio carries foreign-language religious news programmes at various times during the day. Shortwave radio reception is excellent throughout the night and part of the day. British (BBC), American (VOA) and Canadian (CBC) programmes are easily obtained on modest transistor radios. After dark, the American Armed Forces Network (AFN) from Frankfurt or Munich can be heard on regular AM radio (middle or medium wave). RAI television broadcasts only in Italian.

R   **RELIGIOUS SERVICES** *(funzione religiosa)*. Roman Catholic mass is normally celebrated only in Italian, but confessions are heard every day in English, French, German and Spanish at Venice's Basilica di San Marco during the tourist season. Some towns have non-Catholic services; consult the telephone directory under "Chiese di Altri Culti" to enquire on denominations and times of service, or check with your hotel receptionist. There are Protestant churches in Venice, Udine, Trieste, Cattolica and Ravenna. Synagogues are located in Venice, Ancona, Ferrara, Senigallia, Trieste and Urbino.

S   **SIESTA.** Italians take their siesta period seriously, and just about everything shuts down between 1 and 4 p.m.—and even longer in the heat of the summer. The best thing to do is take a long lunch, a nap, and adapt to the Mediterranean rhythm of life. Conversely, if you can stand the heat, monuments and other unenclosed points of interest will be free of tourists during the siesta period.

T   **TIME DIFFERENCES.** Italy follows Central European Time (GMT +1), and from late March to September clocks are put one hour ahead (= GMT+ 2).

Summer time chart:

New York	London	**Italy**	Jo'burg	Sydney	Auckland
6 a.m.	11 a.m.	**noon**	noon	8 p.m.	10 p.m.

What time is it?   **Che ore sono?**

TIPPING. Though a service charge is added to most restaurant bills, it is customary to leave an additional tip. It is also in order to hand the bellboys, doormen, hat check attendants, garage attendants, etc., a coin or two for their service.

The chart below gives some suggestions as to what to leave.

Hairdresser / Barber	up to 15%
Lavatory attendant	L. 300
Maid, per day	L. 1,000–2,000
Hotel porter, per bag	L. 1,000

Taxi driver	10%
Tourist guide	10%
Waiter	10%

TOILETS. You'll find public toilets in most museums and galleries; restaurants, bars, cafés and large stores are all required to have facilities, as are airports and train stations. You'll also find toilets at service stations along the motorways. They may be designated in different ways: W.C. (for water closet) with the picture of a man or woman; sometimes the wording will be in Italian—*Uomini* (men) or *Donne* (women). The most confusing label for foreigners is *Signori* (men—with a final *i*) and *Signore* (women—with a final *e*).

Where are the toilets? **Dove sono i gabinetti?**

TOURIST INFORMATION OFFICES. The Italian State Tourist Offices (*Ente Nazionale Italiano per il Turismo*, abbreviated E.N.I.T.) are found in Italy and abroad. They publish detailed brochures with up-to-date information on accommodation, means of transport and other general tips and useful addresses for the whole country.

Italian State Tourist Offices:

Australia and New Zealand. E.N.I.T., c/o Alitalia, 118 Alfred Street, Milson Point 2061, Sydney; tel. 2921-555

Canada. 1, Place Ville-Marie, Suite 2414, Montreal H3B 3M9, Que.; tel. (514) 866 7667

Eire. 47, Merrion Square, Dublin 2; tel. (01) 766397

South Africa. E.N.I.T., London House, 21 Loveday Street, P.O. Box 6507, Johannesburg; tel. 838-3247

United Kingdom. 1, Princes Street, London W1R 8AY; tel. (01) 408-1254

U.S.A. 500 N. Michigan Avenue, Chicago, IL 60611; tel. (312) 644-0990
630 Fifth Avenue, New York, NY 110111; tel. (212) 795-5500
St. Francis Hotel, 360 Post Street, San Francisco, CA 94108; tel. (415) 392-6206

T In **Italy**, the E.N.I.T. head office is in:
Via Marghera, 2, Rome; tel. 497 11

Local tourist offices:

Ancona	Via Marcello Marini, 14
	Via Thaon de Revel
Ravenna	Piazza San Francesco, 7
	Via S. Vitale, 2
Rimini	Piazzale Cesare Battisti, 1
	Parco Indipendenza
Trieste	Via Rossini, 6
	Piazza Unità d'Italia
Venice	San Marco, Ascensione, 71c
	Piazzale Roma
	Stazione Santa Lucia (railway station)

Telephone assistance service: The English-speaking operators here will answer your questions and give advice. They also serve as trouble-shooters, offering help to visitors who have problems. Dial 116 anywhere in Italy.

Where's the tourist office?   **Dov'è l'ufficio turistico?**

TRANSPORT

Buses *(autobus)*. Town buses have frequent daytime service, less so at night. Routes are well indicated on signs at every bus stop *(fermata)* and on the vehicles themselves the number, starting point and destination are shown.

Taxis *(tassì* or *taxi)*. Taxis are plentiful all along the coast and may be hailed on the street or at a cab rank. The charge is shown on the meter. The yellow pages list taxis you can call by telephone; these vehicles will arrive with a sum already shown on the meter. Many taxi drivers request you not to smoke.

Because of the constantly rising petrol prices and the delay in adjusting meters, there is usually a supplement added to the meter price. There's also a supplement on night, Sunday and holiday fares, as well as for luggage, and for some airport trips. Check with the hotel receptionist or tourist office on the current prices and supplements. And always negotiate the approximate price in advance for airport trips. Tip about 10%.

Trains *(treno).* Italian trains *try* to run on time as advertised.

The following list describes the various types of service.

TEE	The Trans Europ Express, first class only with surcharge; seat reservations essential.
EuroCity (EC)	International express; first and second class.
Intercity (IC)	Inter-city express with very few stops; a luxury international service with first and second class.
Rapido (R)	Long-distance express train stopping at major cities only; first and second class.
Espresso (EXP)/ Direttissimo	Long-distance train, stopping at main stations.
Diretto (D)	Slower than the *Espresso,* it makes a number of local stops.
Locale (L)	Local train which stops at almost every station.
Accelerato (A)	Same as a *Locale.*
Littorina	Small diesel train used on short runs.

Carozza ristorante Dining car	*Vagone letto* Sleeping car with individual compartments and washing facilities	*Carozza cuccette* Sleeping berth car (couchette); blankets and pillows	*Bagagliaio* Guard's van (baggage car); normally only registered luggage permitted

Better-class trains almost always have dining-cars which offer wine, beer, mineral water and decent if unimaginative food at reasonable prices. All trains have toilets and washing facilities of varying quality. Lacking a reservation, it's wise to arrive at the station at least 20 minutes before departure to ensure a seat: Italy's trains are often very crowded.

The Italian State Railways offer fare reductions in certain cases, particularly for large families. Enquire on discounts at your travel agency.

T

Where's the nearest bus stop/taxi rank?	**Dov'è la fermata d'autobus più vicina/il posteggio di tassì più vicino?**
When's the next bus/train to …?	**Quando parte il prossimo autobus/treno per …?**
I want a ticket to …	**Vorrei un biglietto per …**
single (one-way)	**andata**
return (round-trip)	**andata e ritorno**
first/second class	**prima/seconda classe**
Will you tell me when to get off?	**Può dirmi quando devo scendere?**
What's the fare to …	**Qual è la tariffa per …**

W **WATER.** You need have no fear of drinking the tap water on the Adriatic coast. If water is not drinkable, there should be a warning sign: *acqua non potabile*.

With meals, take wine and/or bottled mineral water. Mineral waters are popularly believed to help not only digestion, but an incredible array of afflictions, and there's certainly something to it.

I'd like a bottle of mineral water.	**Vorrei una bottiglia di acqua minerale.**
fizzy (carbonated)/still	**gasata/naturale**

NUMBERS

0	zero	12	dodici	31	trentuno
1	uno	13	tredici	32	trentadue
2	due	14	quattordici	40	quaranta
3	tre	15	quindici	50	cinquanta
4	quattro	16	sedici	60	sessanta
5	cinque	17	diciassette	70	settanta
6	sei	18	diciotto	80	ottanta
7	sette	19	diciannove	90	novanta
8	otto	20	venti	100	cento
9	nove	21	ventuno	101	centouno
10	dieci	22	ventidue	500	cinquecento
11	undici	30	trenta	1000	mille

NUMBERS

SOME USEFUL EXPRESSIONS

yes/no	**sì/no**
please/thank you	**per favore/grazie**
excuse me/you're welcome	**mi scusi/prego**
where/when/how	**dove/quando/come**
how long/how far	**quanto tempo/quanto dista**
yesterday/today/tomorrow	**ieri/oggi/domani**
day/week/month/year	**giorno/settimana/mese/anno**
left/right	**sinistra/destra**
up/down	**su/giù**
good/bad	**buono/cattivo**
big/small	**grande/piccolo**
cheap/expensive	**buon mercato/caro**
hot/cold	**caldo/freddo**
old/new	**vecchio/nuovo**
open/closed	**aperto/chiuso**
free (vacant)/occupied	**libero/occupato**
near/far	**vicino/lontano**
early/late	**presto/tardi**
quick/slow	**rapido/lento**
full/empty	**pieno/vuoto**
easy/difficult	**facile/difficile**
right/wrong	**giusto/sbagliato**
here/there	**qui/là**

Does anyone here speak English?	**C'è qualcuno che parla inglese?**
I don't understand.	**Non capisco.**
Please write it down.	**Lo scriva, per favore.**
Waiter/Waitress, please.	**Cameriere!/Cameriera!**
I'd like …	**Vorrei …**
How much is that?	**Quant'è?**
Have you something less expensive?	**Ha qualcosa di meno caro?**
What time is it?	**Che ore sono?**
Just a minute.	**Un attimo.**
Help me, please.	**Per favore, mi aiuti.**

Index

An asterisk (*) next to a page number indicates a map reference. For index to Practical Information, see inside front cover.